The ... iness

D0235114

WITHDRAWN

The Book of Happiness

Brilliant Ideas to Transform Your Life

Heather Summers and Anne Watson

CAPSTONE

Copyright © 2006 by Heather Summers and Anne Watson

The right of Heather Summers and Anne Watson to be identified as the authors of this book has been asserted in accordance with the Copyright, Designs and Patents Act 1988

First published 2006 by
Capstone Publishing Limited (a Wiley Company)
The Atrium
Southern Gate
Chichester
West Sussex
PO19 8SQ
www.wileyeurope.com
Email (for orders and customer service enquires): cs-books@wiley.co.uk

All Rights Reser   a retrieval system
or transmitted in   **NEWCASTLE UPON TYNE**   pying, recording,
scanning or othe   **CITY LIBRARIES**   atents Act 1988 or
under the terms   Tottenham Court
Road, London V   er. Requests to the
Publisher shoul   ons Ltd, The Atrium, Southern G   **C288582600**   o permreq@wiley.
co.uk, or faxed t

Bertrams	29.07.06
152.42	£9.99

Designations u: ed as trademarks.
All brand name   vice marks, trademarks or regist   ot associated with
any product or

This publicatio   on in regard to the
subject matter covered. It is sold on the understanding that the Publisher is not engaged in rendering professional services. If professional advice or other expert assistance is required, the services of a competent professional should be sought.

CIP catalogue records for this book are available from the British Library and the US Library of Congress

ISBN-13: 978-1-84112-702-6
ISBN-10: 1-84112-702-7

Internal illustrations by G O'Byrne

Typeset in 12/14 pt Palatino by Sparks, Oxford – www.sparks.co.uk
Printed and bound in Great Britain by TJ International Ltd, Padstow, Cornwall
This book is printed on acid-free paper responsibly manufactured from sustainable forestry in which at least two trees are planted for each one used for paper production.

About the Authors

Heather Summers is an experienced senior executive who now runs her own successful human resources and management consultancy business. As well as strategic consultancy she specialises in executive coaching, personal growth coaching and training. Heather believes we all have much more potential than we give ourselves credit for. All the training that she is involved in, including the Luck Workshops she runs with Anne Watson, help people find and fulfil that potential.

Heather holds an MBA, has an MA in English Literature and French, is qualified in Psychometrics and is a Master Practitioner in NLP. She is married with two children and lives in Harrogate.

 **Anne Watson** runs an executive search business that focuses on finding high-achieving executives for businesses, and works with teams to ensure that they achieve their potential. In 1998 she sold a successful business, gaining the freedom to work in those areas that she is most passionate about. This includes running Luck Workshops with Heather Summers and challenging participants to take charge of their own destiny and outperform their own expectations. She has an MA Hons in Hispanic Languages, speaks four other languages including Urdu, is a qualified psychometrician and is a Master Practitioner in NLP. She is married with two children and divides her time between London and Harrogate.

To contact the authors, please email them at:

Heather@switchtosuccess.co.uk
Anne@switchtosuccess.co.uk

Alternatively, you can visit www.switchtosuccess.co.uk

Acknowledgements

We are very happy to acknowledge that we have had huge fun writing this book and that we were encouraged and helped by many people along the way. We are very grateful to everyone who has visited our website www.switchtosuccess.co.uk and filled in the Happiness Questionnaire, thus helping us with our research. We were delighted that so many people took the trouble to get in touch and offer us their personal stories and experiences.

John Moseley, Commissioning Editor of Wiley, and Iain Campbell, Marketing Manager, have supported us throughout with their professionalism and with their humour – what a powerful combination! Scott Smith from Wiley was the source of irrepressible inventiveness as well as having a song for every occasion.

The team at Lancaster University, Amelia Johnson, Angela Burns, Louisa Hebb and Laura Richmond, did a sterling job of the research, providing thought-provoking findings for us to develop.

So many others helped us along the way with their willingness to talk to us about happiness. Other help was gratefully received from people including Sheila Fraser, Janet Orgill, Margaret-Anne Clark, Frances Kittles, Christiane Riffaud, Laura and Mark Williams, Polly Evans, Laura Marks, Tom and Eleanor Hawkins and Terry Carroll.

Martin Hawkins prevented our skilful creative avoidance techniques by keeping us supplied with food and coffee and, lastly, Herbert the Briard again stuck to us throughout, an example to us all with his ability to enjoy happiness in the moment.

Contents

Creating an environment that will increase your happiness

- ❖ What we mean by Surroundings
- ❖ How your Surroundings affect your happiness
- ❖ Brilliant Ideas for improving your Surroundings and growing the Happiness Habit
- ❖ Workbook – practical actions you can take to increase the amount of happiness in your Surroundings. Take the Happiness Challenge!

work for you and which will result in happiness.
Take the Happiness Challenge!

7 Identity - Be Yourself

Being yourself – seeing yourself for who you are and using
this knowledge to get the happiness you truly deserve

- ❖ What we mean by Identity
- ❖ How your Identity affects your happiness
- ❖ Brilliant Ideas for getting to know who you
  are and to be happy within yourself
- ❖ Workbook – practical actions you can take to
  increase the amount of happiness resulting from
  being true to yourself. Take the Happiness Challenge!

8 Purpose

Being more than yourself – finding the path to the Purpose
and meaning in your life

- ❖ What we mean by Purpose
- ❖ How your Purpose affects your happiness
- ❖ Brilliant Ideas for finding your Purpose in life
  and feeling happy about why you are here
- ❖ Workbook – practical actions you can take to
  set a course for happiness in your life. Take
  the Happiness Challenge!

Introduction

Most people aspire to being happier than they already are. They want to experience more enjoyment, more laughter, more pleasure, more success in life, work and relationships. However good it is, it could be better.

This book tells you how you can increase the amount of happiness in your life.

Start by filling in the Happiness Questionnaire either in Chapter 1 of this book or on-line at www.switchtosuccess.co.uk. This will give you an instant snapshot of your current state of happiness and you can use this to help you decide which critical aspects of happiness you need to focus on.

Our research shows us that those people who consider themselves to be most happy believe that happiness is a choice and a habit. We also know that it only takes 21 days to get rid of an unwanted habit and to acquire a new one. Just think of that – 21 days from now your life will be transformed! You will have decided that you control your own destiny and your own level of happiness. Not only that, you will have read the hundreds of Brilliant Ideas that you can adopt to help you get there. You will feel new energy and new enthusiasm for life. You will reappraise the critical elements that make up your life such as your job, your

relationships, your health, your money, your lifestyle and where you live. Make your starting point the belief that you could be happier and then this book will work brilliantly for you.

It is impossible to look at happiness without also considering unhappiness. A lot of our potential for happiness is reduced, restricted or even sabotaged by unnecessary unhappiness. You will learn in the course of this book many strategies for reducing unhappiness.

When we talk about happiness we don't mean euphoria, although that is a part of happiness, nor do we mean pleasure for pleasure's sake. It is making the most of what we have at each moment in time. This habit stops us from always postponing the moment when we believe we will be happy. Instead of constantly projecting happiness into a future time and place, 'when I retire', 'when I graduate', 'when I have paid off my mortgage', 'when I meet the person of my dreams', 'when I win the lottery', 'when I have travelled the world', 'when I have a family', 'when my children grow up', happiness will always be now. This skill of learning to live in the happy, present moment will also give you a bank of happy memories. These memories, just like photographs and videos/DVDs will provide happiness in the future and will be a brilliant resource to draw on when you are facing tough times or unhappy situations.

This book has been built on a solid foundation of research. Thousands of people have filled in our Happiness Questionnaire on www.switchtosuccess.co.uk. We have used this data to analyse the true nature of happiness and to use a model that describes how you can build happiness at six different levels.[1]

We were assisted in our research by the Innovation and Enterprise Unit of Lancaster University. They conducted an analysis of whether different age groups have different beliefs around what constitutes happiness.

Important findings across all age groups were as follows.

❖ Good health does not give you happiness but poor health makes you unhappy, whether it is yours or someone else's.
❖ Comparing ourselves to others affects our happiness. Generally people compare themselves unfavourably with others. They look at who they are and what they have and this comparison leads to feelings of unhappiness and discontent.
❖ Having more and more possessions does not increase happiness. It simply makes us want more.
❖ The most powerful source of happiness is human contact, whether it is with friends, family or closer relationships.

One surprising but wonderfully British finding, was that weather impacts more on people than you could ever imagine. The research showed that bad weather was a strong influence on how people felt and could go a long way towards explaining why so many British people own a place in the sun.

A salient difference between the age groups related to attitude to money. Younger people thought that money made them happy whereas older people thought that money was not a significant factor when thinking of happiness.

The research also demonstrated very clearly that youthful optimism is gradually eroded and as people get older, they become less happy. This is caused by people allowing themselves to be affected by things outside their control. We, on the other hand, believe that happiness comes from within and that we have control over it. Whatever age you are you can choose how to look at circumstances and events in such a way as to increase happiness. Rather than allowing yourself to be swept along by events, emotions and experiences, decide now that happiness is inside you and within your control.

All of this goes to show that there is no natural entitlement to happiness. It means different things to different people. Nonetheless the structure of happiness remains the same for all of us. It does not arrive on a plate but needs to be developed, worked at and grown. We believe that by understanding the six steps on the Stairway of Happiness and by using the self knowledge gained from the Happiness Questionnaire you will be able use the Brilliant Ideas in a very practical way. *The Book of Happiness* will show you how to change any unhelpful attitudes and responses to ones that will transform your life. Make sure you enjoy yourself along the way!

[1] The concept of logical levels of learning and change was initially formulated as a mechanism in the behavioural sciences by Gregory Bateson, based on the work of Bertrand Russell in logic and mathematics. The term 'logical levels', as it is used in NLP (Neuro Linguistic Programming), was adapted from Bateson's work by Robert Dilts in the mid 1980s and refers to hierarchy of levels of processes with an individual or group. We have used this thinking as part of the inspiration for our Stairway of Happiness.

If you mainly agree, tick YES.

If you mainly disagree, tick NO.

Answer every question and remember that although some answers may be harder to find than others, the more honest you are, the more valid the results will be.

Don't spend too long over any one question. If you are undecided, it's important to put down the first answer that popped into your mind.

The Happiness Questionnaire

How happy can you be? Before you can take any steps to increase your happiness, it's best to check how happy you are right now.

We may or may not be born with a natural flair for happiness, but everyone can make or increase their own happiness in different parts of their life. It is simply a question of knowing how. Fill in the questionnaire below before you read the book and discover how truly happy you think you are.

When filling in this questionnaire, first of all remember that there are no right or wrong answers, with nothing bad or good about any score. Use the results to decide how you are going to read the book. Remember that this will be a reflection of how you are choosing to be at this particular moment in time. You can change if you want to and if you are willing to learn how to change.

You can also do this Happiness Questionnaire on our website www.switchtosuccess.co.uk. If you take the time to do that as well, then you will receive by e-mail an individually tailored Happiness Profile.

Overleaf you will find 36 statements. Read each statement carefully and decide whether you agree with it more than you disagree.

		Yes	No
1	I love where I live and work	☑	☑
2	I wish I was happier with what is going on in my life	☑	☐
3	I get out and about to places I want to be	☑	☐
4	The key relationships in my life are not how I want them to be	☑	☐
5	Many of the people I mix with drain my energy	☐	☑
6	I love the sights and sounds that surround me daily	☑	☐
7	When things go wrong I remember happy times	☐	☑
8	I make time for the things that give me pleasure	☑	☑
9	What I do in my daily life at home or work sometimes gets me down	☑	☑
10	I enjoy many different interests that fill my life	☑	☐
11	I know I could take better care of myself	☑	☐
12	I talk nicely to myself and to other people	☑	☐
13	I feel I could make much more of the talents I have	☑	☐
14	I like to learn new things	☑	☐
15	I know I am always improving	☑	☑
16	I find it difficult to change myself at times	☑	☑
17	I tend to assume that I am not good at many things	☑	☐
18	I use my imagination and my mind to develop myself	☑	☑
19	Sometimes I struggle to get up in the morning	☑	☐
20	I believe life will go my way	☑	☑
21	I value the people in my life	☑	☐
22	I know what is important to me	☑	☐

		Yes	No
23	I tend to take the good things I have for granted	☑	☐
24	I know I can tackle anything life throws at me	☐	☑
25	I am happy with my roots	☑	☐
26	Sometimes I wonder if I really matter	☑	☐
27	There are times when I wonder who I am	☐	☑
28	I am a worthwhile person	☑	☐
29	I am glad that I am who I am	☑	☐
30	Knowing who I am makes me happy	☐	☑
31	I am unsure where I am going in life	☑	☐
32	Life is meaningful	☑	☐
33	I sometimes feel out of step with the world	☑	☐
34	I feel part of a larger whole	☐	☑
35	My contribution will last	☐	☑
36	I am able to let go of things that really don't matter	☑	☐

The Stairway of Happiness Scoring Grid

Transfer every answer (Yes or No) into the relevant box in the Scoring Grid below. Score one point for every answer you have that appears in a shaded box.

Then add up your totals.

							Totals
1	2	3	4	5	6	Step 1 – *Surroundings*	3.
7	8	9	10	11	12	Step 2 – *Behaviour*	3 2
13	14	15	16	17	18	Step 3 – *Skills and Capabilities*	1 3
19	20	21	22	23	24	Step 4 – *Values and Beliefs*	2 4
25	26	27	28	29	30	Step 5 – *Identity*	3 4
31	32	33	34	35	36	Step 6 – *Purpose*	2 3

In order to understand your scores, check out the Stairway of Happiness below, then go on to read how to interpret your scores.

The Stairway of Happiness

Step 6 – Purpose
Purpose is what brings meaning into your life. It's why you are here.

Step 5 – Identity
Identity is about acknowledging your roots and accepting yourself for who you are.

Step 4 – Values and Beliefs
Values and Beliefs are the programming, power, motivation and energy behind your actions.

Step 3 – Skills and Capabilities
Skills and Capabilities are all the talents you have or could have, given the opportunity.

Step 2 – Behaviour
Behaviour includes what you do, how you do it, who you do it with and how others behave with you. It's also about what you think, what you say and how you say it.

Step 1 – Surroundings
Your Surroundings are everything you see, hear and feel when you look around you. It's your environment and the results you are getting.

Interpreting your scores on the Stairway of Happiness

Each row on the Scoring Grid represents one of the Steps on the Stairway of Happiness. The person who is truly happy is someone who sustains a high score at every level.

When you look at the scores you will see that the maximum score on any of the Steps is 6. If you have scored 4 or more, it would indicate that you are reasonably happy at that level. However, a score of 3 or less could mean that you have a certain dissatisfaction in that area of your life.

In order to improve the amount of happiness in your life, begin by reading the full description of each of the Steps on the Stairway of Happiness. First of all focus on all the parts of your life that bring you happiness. It is important to keep these in mind and to appreciate them before focusing on those areas where you have the lowest score. Now you can begin your journey of exploration. Remember that how you feel today about your happiness may differ from what you felt last week or what you may feel next week. Use the techniques and the Brilliant Ideas in each chapter of *The Book of Happiness* to make that state more permanent.

The Stairway of Happiness

Step 1 - Surroundings

Your Surroundings are everything you see, hear and feel when you look around you. This includes your physical environment at home and at work. It's the places that you visit regularly, the weather and the climate you live in. It's the places you don't visit, the places you don't go and the things that you don't have as well as the things you do. It's what you see when you look out of your window, it's what you hear, whether it's a bird song or traffic noise. It's what you listen to by choice and what you are forced to listen to. It can be the music you hear or television programmes you watch. It's also about the sort of relationships that surround you and your general health. All these aspects of our environment are the building blocks for our happiness.

Step 2 - Behaviour

What we mean by Behaviour includes what you do, how you do it, who you do it with and how others behave with you. It's also about what you say and how you say it. It's about the recognition that what you do and what you say has an impact on how happy you feel. This is not only what you say out loud to others but it's your internal voice whispering in your ear. Behaviour is about choice. It's about taking responsibility for your own actions and the way you respond to the situations that you have to deal with every day in life. This includes your attitude and your emotional responses. It's whether you tap into your good memories or focus on the bad things that have happened in the past.

Step 3 - Skills and Capabilities

Skills and Capabilities cover a very wide range. This is not just about examination success, formal qualifications or certificates, badges or medals that prove your worth. It includes a huge range of skills which you are capable of growing if you put your mind to it or if you have the opportunity. It is how you manage your emotions and your behaviours. Some skills come naturally and others need working at. It encompasses how you manage your physical well-being and health, ensuring you are in the best possible state to make the most of your natural gifts. By growing your gifts, you grow the happiness habit.

Step 4 - Values and Beliefs

Values and Beliefs are the programming, the power and the motivation for what we do in our daily lives. They provide the energy and the drive and the passion behind our actions. Our values are the things that are important to us. This can include things such as harmony, security, health, freedom, honesty, trust, family, generosity, openness, cleanliness, orderliness, organisation, variety, impulsiveness, options – the list is endless and it's also personal. Beliefs are our truths. They can be our guidelines, our rules or our justification for the things we do. Living life in line with our values is essential for happiness.

Step 5 - Identity

As a happy person you will know yourself inside and out and accept who you are. You will know your strengths and also the areas that let you down.

Being able to be yourself springs from a certainty and an acceptance about the essence of you. Your Identity is not affected by the labels other people might want to attach to you. Part of who you are lies in your roots – your name, your country, your genes, your upbringing, your loyalties, your country of origin, your faith, the colour of your skin. But it's also about recognising that you are more than that. It's an acceptance that there are many things about yourself that you can't change, and an acknowledgement that you do not have to be imprisoned by them. You can make the most of who you are. The key to being comfortable about your Identity is recognising the qualities you have within you that make you different and unique.

Step 6 - Purpose

Purpose is what brings meaning into your life and the recognition that you are part of a larger whole. It answers the big life question 'Why am I here?' Some people are born with a conviction about the sort of vocation they would like to follow. They have a calling in life and this gives them a personal life map that provides them with a strong direction. If you have a clear sense of Purpose, you are likely to be happy and to integrate successfully your dreams into your life. Those who lack Purpose can find they are restless, aimless or feel dissatisfied with their lives.

The Stairway of Happiness

'And they all lived happily ever after.' The end of the fairy tale is the beginning of life and this is where we are picking up the tale. A fairy tale assumes that happiness is an automatic follow on and an automatic right. Undiluted happiness in a cloudless sky with none of the problems of everyday life to cast a shadow – that's the world of fairy tales.

The fairy-tale version of happiness does not match reality as most of us know it. Happiness comes and goes; sometimes it is more intense than others. Unhappiness can overshadow your life and it can infiltrate all areas. It can prevent you from experiencing pleasure. For example, if you are unhappy you are unlikely to appreciate many of the little things that would normally brighten your day such as the sun shining, or a special meal, the flowers in the window box, music on the radio, the company of a good friend. What is making you unhappy overshadows everything else in your life. It gains a momentum and an importance that is often disproportionate. Sadness is different to unhappiness. Sadness is part of life and we experience it as a result of difficult life events such as bereavement.

If only we had a formula for happiness we could increase our level of happiness and decrease our level of unhappiness.

How would it be if you could have more control over how happy you are day to day, week to week, month to month and year to year?

This book is the best investment of your life but only if you follow our formula for it and commit to the actions we suggest. It takes 21 days to change a habit so think how happy you will be in three weeks time.

Anthony lives in a new second-floor flat. One day he called his friend Howard and asked him if he would help him transport a wardrobe that he was going to buy in IKEA back to his flat and carry it up the stairs, as there was no lift in the building. They went to IKEA together and brought back the wardrobe, which was in typical IKEA flat-pack style.

Howard said he would be glad to do it in exchange for a pint but made it very clear that he was not a natural DIY person and was allergic to flat packs. He said he would help him get the flat pack into the room and then the rest was up to him. Anthony agreed.

A week later Howard called Anthony and asked if his wardrobe was all right. Anthony said, 'It's not up yet.' Howard asked why not and he said, 'Well it says on the box "self assembly" and nothing has happened so far.'

You will find it is just the same with this book. Happiness does not assemble itself automatically. All the components are here for you to construct your own happiness.

There are six clearly identifiable and separate Steps to happiness, which make up the Stairway of Happiness. Each Step is separate and unique; however, each is linked to all the others like all stairways. The reason for being on a stairway is because you are going somewhere. In this case your ultimate destination is happiness. By understanding what happiness means at each Step and by taking action to address the personal issues you identify, you will be using your own personal power to take control of and build your own happiness. This is not a moving escalator. To reach where you want to go you have to keep moving and that requires energy and effort.

To increase your happiness or decrease your unhappiness, you need to do more than read a good book. Being happy includes getting rid of the attitudes and habits that are getting in your way. The Stairway of Happiness will help you identify those areas that you need to change and will show you how you can go about it.

In addition, by using our Brilliant Ideas and the Workbook included in each chapter you will find hundreds of different ways to appreciate and make the most of all the things that already form part of your overall happiness. An exciting 21 days lie ahead – increased happiness is on the horizon.

The Stairway of Happiness

> **Step 6 – Purpose**
> Purpose is what brings meaning into your life. It's why you are here.

> **Step 5 – Identity**
> Identity is about acknowledging your roots and accepting yourself for who you are.

> **Step 4 – Values and Beliefs**
> Values and Beliefs are the programming, power, motivation and energy behind your actions.

> **Step 3 – Skills and Capabilities**
> Skills and Capabilities are all the talents you have or could have, given the opportunity.

> **Step 2 – Behaviour**
> Behaviour includes what you do, how you do it, who you do it with and how others behave with you. It's also about what you think, what you say and how you say it.

> **Step 1 – Surroundings**
> Your Surroundings are everything you see, hear and feel when you look around you. It's your environment and the results you are getting.

You don't have to climb the Stairway from the bottom up. You can start where you want and read the chapters in any order. As you have already done the Happiness Questionnaire in Chapter 1 or the online version on our website www.switchtosuccess. co.uk you will have an idea of where you can make the greatest strides in the shortest time. You will have already have read the full definition of each Step at the end of Chapter 1. Use this to decide your starting point.

People on the Steps

Step 1 - Surroundings

Louise

> Your Surroundings are everything you see, hear and feel when you look around you. It's your environment and the results you're getting.

After 23 years of marriage, Louise's parents suddenly separated and divorced. The family home was sold and her parents each had a smaller flat, her mother in her home town and her father 50 miles away. Louise was extremely upset by the split and although she had the choice of living with either parent, she decided to leave school. She found a job in a hotel 150 miles away and was given a small room in an annexe of the hotel. The change from living in a family home was traumatic. She missed the family meals, the relaxing atmosphere of the house and all the comforts of home. She was miserable.

Because of her difficulty in adjusting to the radical change in her Surroundings, Louise is unhappy. She needs to do something differently as the situation is unlikely to change of its own accord. In order to change she needs to move to Step 2 on the Stairway of happiness and take some action.

Step 2 - Behaviour

Philip

> Behaviour includes what you do, how you do it, who you do it with and how others behave with you. It's also about what you think, what you say and how you say it.

Philip taught English at the local comprehensive school. He had moved into teaching straight from college, sure that he would love the job and make a difference to young people's lives. Fourteen years later he was disenchanted and disillusioned. Money was tight and he was struggling to maintain his wife and two children. Every day he dreaded going to work, feeling he was making no difference. All he was doing was working longer hours and getting more stressed.

He hated his job. He felt he had no choice but to continue as a teacher to pay the mortgage. He was not qualified to do anything else. He had to continue.

If Philip does nothing to change his behaviour, he will be sentenced to a lifetime in a job he now loathes. He runs the risk of ill health, depression and unhappiness.

In order to change his circumstances, perhaps Philip needs to look at the Step above and assess what skills and capabilities he has and see what opportunities they might offer to change his life and increase his happiness.

Step 3 - Skills

Ben

> Skills and Capabilities are all the talents you have, or could have, given the opportunity.

Ben comes from a good home with loving parents. He left school with good exam results and his parents fully expected him to go on and get a good job. He decided to take a year out to go travelling. He went off backpacking round Australia, working in bars and having fun. One year stretched to two, this time going to South America, living on a shoe string and finding life a little tougher. When he got back home, he got a job in a supermarket and was saving to go off to the Far East for another year.

16

Ben was in perpetual motion. Was he happy? When asked, Ben simply said that he felt restless. He knew he had many skills that would get him a well paid job but something was holding him back. Ben had never really tested himself and found out what he was capable of. None of the jobs he had done stretched him so he had lost the confidence to aim higher. It was easier to carry on as he was. In order to change he would need to look at the Step above to find out which of his beliefs and attitudes was holding him back.

Step 4 - Beliefs

Joanne

> Values and beliefs are the programming, power, motivation and energy behind your actions.

Joanne had an unhappy childhood and married young, delighted to escape from her home. Her husband Rob was good looking, had a good job and was fun to be around. It was after the birth of her last child that the violence started. At first it was only verbal abuse but it soon escalated into punches and kicks. Rob told her often that that she was hopeless and a failure and she believed it to be true. Her close friends urged her to leave and take the children with her but she never did. It was not a question of courage; Joanne somehow believed that it was her fault and therefore perhaps violence was part and parcel of the relationship. She did not value herself highly. This belief would have to change if she was to assert herself and her own rights. This could only be done by moving one Step up on the Stairway of Happiness to feel good about herself and who she was.

Step 5 - Identity

Michael

> Identity is about acknowledging your roots and accepting your-
> self for who you are.

Michael had known from a very early age that he was adopted. He loved his adoptive parents dearly yet he was different from them in so many ways. They were both quiet bookish types whereas he was a practical person who loved sport and mixing with people. As time went on he felt the need to discover his genetic roots to find out who he really was.

After months of investigations he eventually tracked down his mother. They met in a coffee bar and the meeting was stilted and difficult. She would not tell him who his father was and refused to allow him to come anywhere near the life she had built for herself. He came away rejected and more confused that ever about who he really was. Despite a good career, a lovely home and supportive family, he felt that life had no meaning. It was as though he was cast adrift, rootless. In order to find meaning in life and to feel that he belongs, he will need to look at the next Step up and find a sense of Purpose.

Step 6 - Purpose

> Purpose is what brings meaning into your life. It's why you are
> here.

Mother Teresa of Calcutta had a purpose. She pursued every avenue to follow what she never doubted was the direction God was pointing. When she won the Nobel Prize in 1979, she said in her acceptance speech, 'I chose the poverty of our poor people. But I am grateful to receive (the Nobel) in the name of the hungry, the naked, the homeless, of the crippled, of the blind, of the lepers, of all those people who feel unwanted, unloved, uncared-for throughout society, people that have become a burden to society and are shunned by everyone.'

Because she had a sense of purpose that drove her in her life, the other Steps on the Stairway of Happiness worked really well. She had a clear sense of Identity. She lived her life in line with her values and beliefs. She made the most of her skills and talents. Her actions were in harmony with her purpose and the results she achieved were the ones she wanted.

The secret of true happiness is for all of the Steps to work together in harmony.

We are not suggesting that you need to be a Mother Teresa, but feeling that there is Purpose in your life will bring you ownership of the Stairway of Happiness.

Working at the next Step up

The individual Steps that form part of the formula for happiness are described in the chapters that follow. We describe the meaning of each Step and put forward Brilliant Ideas to grow the Happiness Habit. It is important to keep in your mind at all times that if what you are doing on one of the Steps does not seem to be increasing your happiness, the answer could lie in one or more of the Steps above. Meaningful and lasting change may therefore only be achieved by working at least one Step above the one you are on.

If what you are doing does not increase your happiness, you need to make changes at least one Step above on the Stairway of Happiness.

So in summary, you need to work at least one Step above the one you are on if ...

- ❖ nothing seems to change, despite the efforts you make
- ❖ things change for a while and then revert to your previous unwanted patterns of behaviour
- ❖ you are not motivated to change even if you know intellectually and logically that you should
- ❖ you don't know what's stopping you from changing, improving or being happier.

Here is an illustration of how this works in practice on each Step.

Stairway of Happiness	How to make changes at the Step above
Step 1 – Surroundings In order to make lasting change in the tings you are not happy about in your Surroundings, you may need to work at least one Step above on the Stairway of Happiness. For example, if you are not happy with the state of your garden or yard, then don't just complain about it, take action to change it. You will then be working at the Behaviour Step. What you are doing now will be different to the sort of habits or inaction you have got accustomed to in the past. Your Behaviour will be different and therefore the results in your Surroundings will be different and better. You will feel happier	**If you need to work at Step 2 – Behaviour – here are some examples.** ❖ Take action and clear rubbish in your yard or garden. ❖ Get cuttings from friends or neighbours and plant. ❖ Read gardening books. ❖ Buy seeds and plant them in pots. **Resulting change in Surroundings:** ❖ A lovely clean and flower-filled yard
Step 2 – Behaviour If you are unhappy with the things you are currently doing, and you want to change them, you may need to work at least one Step above on the Stairway of Happiness – i.e. on the Skills and Capabilities Step. So for example, if you are not getting the results you want from your exercise, you may need to learn what activities would work best for you to get you to the level of fitness you desire. This could be learning a new sport – or increasing your skill in an existing activity. Notice that when you take action, it has an impact on your Surroundings – in this example, your health and feelings of fitness.	**If you need to work at Step 3 – Skills and Capabilities – here are some examples.** ❖ Learn a new exercise routine. ❖ Go jogging further and further each day to build up stamina and fitness capabilities. ❖ Become more skilled in an existing sport by practising more or by going for coaching lessons. **Resulting change in Behaviour:** ❖ You will use your time differently through practising the chosen activities. **Resulting change in Surroundings:** ❖ You will visit new places/meet new people and feel healthier and happier because you are fitter.

Stairway of Happiness	How to make changes at the Step above
Step 3 – Skills and Capabilities If you want to make lasting changes in the number of Skills and Capabilities you have, you may need to make changes at least one Step above on the Stairway of Happiness – i.e. on the Values and Beliefs Step. For example, suppose you would like to learn a new skill such as drawing or painting but you have always been told you are useless at art. This negative belief will either stop you from exploring the options about how you could gain that skill or you may start to learn to draw or paint and then give up sooner rather than later because you believe you are no good. Now if you were to question the belief that you are not good at art, and to start from the assumption that anyone can learn to draw or paint, then there is a far greater likelihood that you will persevere and create some very worthwhile drawings or paintings. Who knows, they may end up not just on your walls but on the walls of an Art Gallery. They may be used as illustrations in books or magazines – or they may simply act as an inspiration to your children or others who share the same limiting belief as you.	**If you need to work at Step 4 – Values and Beliefs – here is an example.** ❖ Replace out-of-date/unhelpful beliefs with practical and positive new ones, e.g., replace 'I believe I can't draw or paint.' with 'I believe I can be good at art.' **Resulting changes in Skills:** ❖ An ability to draw/paint to an acceptable standard. ❖ Learning different drawing or painting techniques. **Resulting changes in Behaviour:** ❖ Attending art classes. ❖ Reading art books and magazines. ❖ Trying out different techniques. ❖ Buying art materials. ❖ Spending time drawing and painting. ❖ Showing your pictures to others and being proud of them. **Resulting changes in Surroundings:** ❖ New framed pictures on the wall, bringing feelings of satisfaction. ❖ Compliments from family and friends. ❖ Watching your children be inspired to create in the ways that are best for them. ❖ Increased confidence overall

Stairway of Happiness	How to make changes at the Step above
Step 4 – Values and Beliefs Sometimes what you believe and what you value (or what you don't believe or what you don't value) will hold you back and contribute to your unhappiness. If you are looking to make lasting change in the sort of values and beliefs you have, then it may be necessary to work one Step up at Step 5 of The Stairway of Happiness – Identity. For instance, if you believe that you are no good at making money, then you need to check out whether you see yourself as a wealthy person or a poor person – and whether you believe in your heart of hearts that it is truly all right for you to have plenty of money. Listen to what you say about yourself, both out loud and in your head. What 'Identity' statements do you make about yourself? For example – you may say things like: 'I am not good with money.' 'I am always short of money.' 'I will never be wealthy.' Once you believe you can make money, there will be no stopping you going out and doing just that. Just think what changes this could make to your Surroundings!	**.If you need to work at Step 5 – Identity – here is an example.** ❖ Try changing any negative or illogical statements you make to more practical and positive ones such as: 'I am good with money.' 'It's OK for me to make a lot more money than I do.' 'It is all right for me to be wealthy.' **Resulting change in Values and Beliefs:** ❖ You believe not only that it's OK for you to make money – that money is not something to feel guilty about achieving – but that you can actually make money. **Resulting changes in Skills and Capabilities:** ❖ You start to learn about the various ways to accumulate wealth and gain some of the necessary knowledge and skills to begin making money. **Resulting changes in Behaviour:** ❖ You find out how others make money and you set some money-making projects in motion. **Resulting changes in Surroundings:** ❖ The things that you always wanted but could never afford begin to come to you – whether they are small things like going away for a weekend, big things like buying a new car, or things that fit your values like giving more to your family or favourite charity

Stairway of Happiness	How to make changes at the Step above
Step 5 – Identity If you are looking to make lasting changes in the sort of image you have about yourself and who you are, you may need to work at the Step above on the Stairway of Happiness – i.e. you need to be clearer about your Purpose in life. This is not as daunting as it might seem. It simply means that you need to be clearer about what sort of things give your life real meaning. For example if you see yourself as someone who is not worth a lot, your self esteem will be low, you are likely to assume that you don't matter and that whatever you do will not make a difference. This will have an impact on the whole of your life and you are likely to have feelings ranging from feelings of dissatisfaction and regret to downright unhappiness. Later on in your life, instead of looking back with satisfaction and pride, you will feel your life has not been worthwhile or that you have not made a difference.	**If you need to work at Step 6 – Purpose – here is an example.** Answer the question 'In what ways am I a worthwhile person?' Make a list of all the things you have done that have brought meaning to your life. Try these on and feel good about the fact that you have already fulfilled part of your Purpose in life. **Resulting change in Identity:** ❖ You will feel better about who you are. **Resulting changes in Values and Beliefs:** ❖ You will value yourself more and believe in yourself. ❖ You will have more confidence in what you have to offer. **Resulting change in Skills and Abilities:** ❖ You will use the talents and abilities you have – and acquire more skills. **Resulting changes in Behaviour:** ❖ You will do more things that will have an impact. ❖ You will take risks and express your views. **Resulting change in Surroundings:** ❖ The world around you will change – people will respond to you more positively and because you will feel you deserve more of the good things in life, you will attract these in your Surroundings.

Stairway of Happiness	How to make changes at the Step above
Step 6 – Purpose This is the top Step on the Stairway of Happiness. As there is no Step above, you may find it useful to consider here the big questions of life – for example: 'What is my Higher Purpose?' 'How do I fit into this world / the universe/ the bigger picture?' 'What else is out there?' If you feel connected to a greater power or a a larger system, you are more likely to know who you are, to feel you have a right to be here, to feel like a worthwhile person and to know the part you will play in the world. This knowledge will affect all the Steps on the Stairway of Happiness and will make you happy.	

HAPPY THOUGHT
The Top Step on the Stairway of Happiness

I know who I am. I have a place and I am a worthwhile person.
I know the part I will play in the world. This knowledge makes
me happy.

3

Surroundings

The First Step on the Stairway of Happiness

This is the first Step on the Stairway of Happiness, the starting point on the journey of happiness. It is a clear, practical place to begin to examine what is right about where you are in life. Now you can ask yourself, 'Am I where I want to be?'

Remember! To make lasting changes to what you don't like in your Surroundings, you may need to work at least one Step above on the Stairway of Happiness. In other words, you may need to take action and change some of the things you do (Behaviour) or increase your Skills and Capabilities, or change your Beliefs or even reassess your Identity or clarify your Purpose.

Step 6 – Purpose
Purpose is what brings meaning into your life. It's why you are here.

Step 5 – Identity
Identity is about acknowledging your roots and accepting yourself for who you are.

Step 4 – Values and Beliefs
Values and Beliefs are the programming, power, motivation and energy behind your actions.

Step 3 – Skills and Capabilities
Skills and Capabilities are all the talents you have or could have, given the opportunity.

Step 2 – Behaviour
Behaviour includes what you do, how you do it, who you do it with and how others behave with you. It's also about what you think, what you say and how you say it.

Step 1 – Surroundings
Your Surroundings are everything you see, hear and feel when you look around you. It's your environment and the results you are getting.

Surroundings

Your Surroundings are everything you see, hear and feel when you look around you. This includes your physical environment at home and at work. Your Surroundings are the places that you visit regularly, the weather and the climate you live in. It's the places you don't visit, the places you don't go and the things that you don't have as well as the things you do. It's what you see when you look out of your window, it's what you hear, whether it's a bird song or traffic noise. It's what you listen to by choice and what you are forced to listen to. It can be the music you hear or television programmes you watch. It's also about the sort of relationships that surround you and your general health. All these aspects of our environment are the building blocks for happiness.

Look around you. How can you be happy …

- ❖ if you are living a place you don't want to be
- ❖ if you are working with people you don't like
- ❖ if your family is causing you pain
- ❖ if you are in a job you hate
- ❖ if you are in a relationship that is making you miserable
- ❖ if you're deeply in debt or worried about money
- ❖ if you are constantly at odds with people
- ❖ if you lack the possessions you most want or need
- ❖ if you can't travel to the places you want to visit
- ❖ if you feel trapped in your home, your work or your relationships
- ❖ if you lack energy, your health is poor
- ❖ if you've lost your sense of fun
- ❖ if everything is an effort?

This chapter is about how to increase your happiness by changing those aspects of your Surroundings that cause you greatest unhappiness.

For some people, their physical environment is really important. They like to be surrounded by lovely sights and sounds; they like to travel to new places and see new things. Others notice their physical environment less but place a high importance on their relationships. Just think for a moment of all the stories you have heard of people marrying for money because they love the Surroundings that money can bring. Equally there are many

ople who have left their wealth and riches behind to
someone they love!

e a moment to register which aspects of your Surround-
are most important to you. A good way to start would be to
ppreciate and focus briefly on the main things around you that
bring you most happiness.

Now look around you and think more deeply about what's
happening out there in your life. How do you feel? Pay attention
to what you see, what you listen to, what you hear – and notice
what you feel. Are things how you want them to be? Are you
getting the results you want in your life? Think about the sort
of people who surround you in your life. Are they the ones you
want? What about where you live – is it where you want to be?
What's happening around you that you like or love – and what's
distressing you?

Let's look at some of the different things that make up your
environment in more detail. This is a bit like doing an MOT test
to find out what's working and what isn't. A good review will
therefore help you appreciate all the good things you have in
your life as well as help you to work out what needs changing.
Of course, there may be some things that it's not possible for you
to change – at least at the moment – but as you do this review,
aim to keep an open mind about what's possible.

The environment we grow up in

The environment we grow up in has a huge effect on our lives
and therefore our happiness. Our experiences in childhood can
set the course for our attitude to life and our inbuilt sense of
happiness or unhappiness. Those aspects of our childhood that
have caused us pain often result in unconscious decisions that
affect our overall direction in life (Purpose), how we feel about
ourselves (Identity) what's important to us and what we hold to
be true (Values and Beliefs), what we feel capable of achieving
(Skills and Capabilities), what we actually do (Behaviour) and

the results that follow in our environment (Surroundings). We come full circle!

Where you live

One of the most important aspects of our life is our home and where we live. Most of us spend a lot of time and money improving our homes and gardens. We introduce colour, comfort, space and light knowing that these will improve our outlook and our spirits. Who wants to live in a dark, bleak basement sitting on an orange box? Television make-over programmes recognise that by improving people's homes and gardens they are improving people's quality of life and increasing their pleasure in their Surroundings. Many different things bring life to your home. Photographs, mementos, flowers, plants, music, pets, tropical fish, paintings and pictures all contribute to comfort and familiarity.

Some people are naturally orderly and other people are chaotic in the way that they live. They just don't notice the clutter or mess and they don't realise that a good clean up or tidy up could have a direct impact on their state of mind. Kim and Aggie, the dust-busting divas from the Channel 4 television programme *How Clean is Your House?*, recognise that restoring order from chaos brings increased satisfaction in personal Surroundings.

It's easy not to recognise the huge impact that where we live has on our health and happiness.

Two for the price of one

Take Janice for instance. She is 40 and recently married for the first time. When single, she lived in a smart town house which she had lovingly furnished and decorated to her taste over a number of years. Her house was in a good area, convenient for her work and near her family. When she married, she and her husband planned to sell both their houses and buy a property between them.

Unfortunately the property market slumped at that time and neither house sold. Janice managed to rent out her property and so she moved into her husband's house – temporarily. This house was in an undesirable area, needed a lot doing to it to make it saleable and was not somewhere Janice felt comfortable.

A year later she was still there. The property market had still not recovered and as she and her husband were keen to get the best price for the property they used the time to make significant improvements.

It took Janice some time to realise that despite the home improvements they had made, despite a loving husband and despite a well paid job, her physical Surroundings were affecting her state of mind. This in turn affected her energy levels and her health. She had convinced herself there was nothing she could do about selling the property in the short term and that the decision they had made was both logical and necessary. One illness or complaint followed another and her energy became so low that she was on the verge of depression.

Once she realised what was happening, she talked about it with her husband. They put both houses back on the market, sold them for less than they had originally wanted, but found a new home that they both loved.

By reassessing her view of what it was possible to change in her environment, Janice found renewed health, energy and happiness.

You may feel perfectly happy with where you live and where you work; you may believe that they are OK but could be better, or you may hate your Surroundings. Wherever you sit on this scale, there is always room for improvement. There is nothing quite like taking stock of where you are and facing up to reality.

So ask yourself – is your home a place you love being in and coming back to – or is it a prison – somewhere you feel trapped, or uncomfortable? If it's not the place you want it to be, check out the Brilliant Ideas at the end of this chapter so that it becomes one of the building blocks to your happiness.

A dream house abroad

Why is it that so many people in the UK have sold up and moved to France or Spain? Over a million British people own a house in France and half a million have moved to Spain. They are following the dream that if they have a lovely mortgage-free house in a pleasant climate, they will be healthier, happier and in possession of that elusive key to personal satisfaction.

What they want to get from a move abroad include things such as …

- ❖ better climate
- ❖ a house with a bigger garden
- ❖ the opportunity to learn another language
- ❖ the chance to experience another culture
- ❖ quality family time together
- ❖ family and friends visiting
- ❖ building a new lifestyle or business, maybe through holiday lets
- ❖ escape from the rat race
- ❖ getting away from the drudgery of routine
- ❖ escape from cold, damp, dark winters
- ❖ wonderful Mediterranean food
- ❖ sitting on terraces soaking up the sun.

For some of these people the dream comes true. Others find only homesickness, loneliness and isolation. They discover the weather is not wonderful throughout the year and the winters are cold. They are surrounded by the unfamiliar sights of a foreign place and they miss the morning paper, Radio 2, night classes, the cinema, Sainsbury's and bumping into friends and acquaintances as they walk down the street.

The language barrier, too, often causes stress, and whereas it can be managed at a market stall buying vegetables, it is magnified when trying to discuss the intricacies of local planning law at the Town Hall or trying to talk to tradespeople about technical or specific building problems. It's interesting that communication is something that we all take for granted and it's doubtful if any of us would consider it to be a critical part of our happiness until it is taken away.

Alhama de Granada is a beautiful Moorish town in Andalusia, half way between Malaga and Granada. It enjoys hot summers and mild winters. It is close to the full restored roman and Moorish 'balnearios', the baths built on hot springs and still providing therapies and treatments today. Alhama de Granada is only half an hour from the coast and offers all the pleasures of Spanish lifestyle and climate.

Keith and Liz now live there with their two children aged 5 and 9, having moved there in the autumn of 2005. The children go to a local school, learning the language and quickly adapting to their new life. Keith and Liz are settling into their new house while they deal with the complications of restoring two other houses that they will probably let out as holiday homes for additional income. Keith and Liz are following their dream and living a life in a place in the sun. Keith is working on his third novel, which he hopes his agent will be able to sell together with the others to a publisher. Now is the time for him to focus on his dream to be a crime novelist while living in a place he loves.

Both Keith and Liz enjoyed successful careers in the UK, Keith in the finance department of an NHS trust and Liz as a lecturer. Keith was unsettled in his role, not believing that it was his true vocation and Liz was concerned about educational cuts. They had often talked about moving to Spain and it took a major health scare for them to decide to do it. They made the decision and acted quickly, deciding on a move to Alhama de Granada as they had visited it before. The only barrier to their happiness is Keith's need to learn Spanish. The key to new friendships and putting roots down in society is the ability to communicate. Once Keith has mastered Spanish he will move beyond the circle of expatriate English people and put down real roots in Spain. By changing their Surroundings they have satisfied their sense of Purpose, Step 6, but they have created a need to be working at Step 3 of the Stairway of Happiness – a need to master the Spanish language, which will open up new vistas of happiness.

Energy and your Surroundings

Each person has an energy that radiates around them. It's a living energy made up of electromagnetic particles, sometimes called an aura. We know auras exist because they can be photographed by a process called Kirlian photography. Our auras are open to exchange with all forms of energy. Just think of the people who drain your energy when you're with them – and others who inspire you and seem to add to your energy. Some events such as conflict or being angry or disappointed may drain you. Other events will make you feel good – such as being with someone you love – and will add to your energy.

We don't just interact with others people and their energy; we also interact with all aspects of our Surroundings that radiate energy – pets, plants, trees, flowers, birds, animals, the weather – all aspects of nature. It is said that different colours have different energies that we respond to and we all know that it feels different in the dark to being in the light and that different lights have different effects on our energies. Low energy results in feeling low, feeling tired and therefore reduces the amount of happiness we have access to. This is one of the key reasons why this first Step on the Stairway of Happiness is such a critical one.

35

Getting out of the trap

Have you ever found that your Surroundings and circumstances have changed in such a way that you feel trapped? A happy marriage and relationship may change into a difficult or unhappy one which it is difficult to escape from. A lively bustling home may change to an empty and lonely house when the children have left. Similarly if a loved partner dies, the house becomes empty and a place of memories only.

You may live in a housing estate surrounded by crime, drug addicts, and poverty and not have the money to leave, or you may feel isolated and trapped in a house in the country or in a new town or country where you know no-one. It may not always be possible to change your Surroundings. If that is the case, perhaps you need to consider how you could be proactive in changing what you do so that your Surroundings become less of a cage. This could range from changing your routines so that you meet more people or go to different places or find like-minded people. If you suddenly find yourself alone, then changing your routines will help reduce the triggers that make you feel your loss so badly.

Sometimes being trapped is a state of mind rather than a reality. So whatever your circumstances, give yourself a choice. Choose to stay or choose to go, no matter what the consequences are.

How we gain self-worth

We gain a real source of self-worth and self-confidence from the people around us we engage with. This can come from anyone we meet along the way – family, friends, colleagues, people on the train or at the checkout at Asda. How we get on with them and how they react to us can make us feel better about life and ourselves. We can recognise the power of this by looking at the reverse side of the coin. Look at the misery caused by conflict or poor relationships, the unhappiness caused by bullying and abuse. This is a consequence of the dark side of relationships, leaving at least one of the parties feeling diminished, unworthy and unhappy.

Good relationships, on the other hand help you confirm that you are an OK and worthwhile person – and that helps you feel good.

Happiness can't be bottled – it's different for everyone

One person's definition of happiness is not usually the same as the next person's. Whereas you might like sitting on a river bank fishing all day with only yourself for company, someone else might love going down Oxford Street loving the noise, the crowds, the hustle and the bustle. If we are to create happiness in others we cannot assume that what makes us happy will have the same effect on them.

You get what you give

Making others happy and giving to others is a great source of happiness for many people. This works well because it follows a universal principle – that overall we get back what we give. Some people, however, fall into the trap of giving to others at the expense of themselves and their own needs. Unless you feed and nurture yourself, you will end up empty, with nothing to give. This will result in you feeling cheated, taken for granted, resentful or even bitter – and with low self-esteem. This is not the path to happiness.

The ups and the downs

Polly Evans would seem to be the envy of us all, enjoying her career as a travel writer. So far her books include *It's not about the Tapas*, a hilarious tale of Polly cycling across seemingly inaccessible parts of Spain on her gleaming Italian bicycle, musing on the history of the places she sees along the way, while she battles with the contemporary issues of survival, finding a place to eat, a place to sleep as well as finding the strength to move on to the next step along the route.

Polly hotly denies that fate has handed her a cushy number, spending half the year on one long holiday and the other half effortlessly turning out pristine prose.

She desperately tries to engage our sympathies by telling us of the hardships and uncertainties of travelling on her own in difficult environments. She describes in graphic detail the stomach-churning encounters with foreign public lavatories, the misery of unappetising and unidentifiable objects served up as food. She tells us of the loneliness of life on the road with no one to talk to. We begin to feel a little sorry for her, enduring all these miseries in order to bring us stories from foreign parts. Then she tells us of the richness of the cultures she encounters, the surprises she finds along the way, and the small glimpses of spectacular beauty in the midst of a long hard day. Her eyes light up when she tells us of the sheer euphoria of galloping hell for leather across wide open spaces in Argentina. She is gleeful as she talks about the iron grip of Mao Tse Tung on a nation, now dubiously embalmed in Tiananmen Square in Beijing. Polly may endure hardship and misery along the way but her gift of doing everything with enthusiasm ensures that ultimately she is happy in what she does. Her Surroundings change according to the project she engages in but all paths lead to her warm, inviting home in London. Polly knows what she is doing and she certainly knows who she is, having a strong sense of responsibility and Purpose. Money and fame are not her goal, although a few extra thousand wouldn't go amiss. She loves her life of constant contrasts and paradoxes. She takes pleasure in the spectacular as well as the simple. Natural beauty such as the sudden lifting of the clouds in the peaks of Huang Sman gives her a sense of happiness and euphoria and yet sometimes she just sits staring admiringly at her fridge, marvelling at the wonder of it.

Polly's sense of humour seems to pull her through those days when she is thoroughly fed up, in a black mood, depressed and in a rage. She realised one day in China that she had gone 10 days without speaking to a soul so she preyed upon unsuspecting foreigners that she spotted in the distance, 'Hi, my name's Polly … '.

Maybe what *we* learnt from Polly is that an essential part of happiness is having a bit of misery along the way. The Polly Evans rocket fuel of enthusiasm, hard work and zest for life is what sees you through the dark moments. She believes herself to be fortunate and needs to give something back. She does not expect the path to be straightforward, which is just as well given her chosen profession, but she does keep pushing, keep working, keep writing. Happiness for Polly is plotting her next journey to the Yukon travelling on dog sleds. She knows there will be tough moments but equally there will be great rewards. She philosophically resigns herself to the occasional tears of loneliness and homesickness but she is spurred on by knowing she is doing what makes her happy.

In recognition of Polly's honesty, I am now publicly prepared to declare that travel writers are not just people on long holidays keeping detailed diaries. Polly may endure more disasters in her working life than most of us, but she probably experiences greater heights. Is this the recipe for enduring happiness, being thankful for the simple and ordinary as well as the euphoric? Better ask Polly.

> Polly Evans is the author of *Fried Eggs with Chopsticks*, *Kiwis Might Fly*, and *It's Not About the Tapas*.

The different kinds of relationships we have

Although we will explore this further on the next Step of the Stairway of Happiness, it is worthwhile examining relationships in the context of your Surroundings and seeing how they impact on your happiness.

Colleagues and people you come across

Colleagues you work with can make your life easier or harder. You can either allow others to drive the quality and nature of your relationships or you can choose to put energy and effort into them to make them work in the best possible way. We're not just talking here about people you know well and who play important parts in your life. We mean the people you may only brush up against once or twice – for example the person in the call centre, the airline check-in staff, the ticket collector on the train, the shop assistant in the department store, the plumber, the waiter, the bar tender, the bank clerk. Maybe you're expecting these people to take the initiative with you and so your expectations are not met. You are disappointed with how they engage with you yet you do not put yourself out to engage with them!

Your close relationships

How are the relationships with your family, friends and life partner? Are they positive, harmonious and relatively conflict-free? If they are, what are you doing to make sure that they stay that way? If they're not and you want them to change, what are you choosing to do about it? Good relationships of any sort need to be worked at and are unlikely to change of their own accord. A lot of unhappiness can be caused by the behaviour of those closest to us ... While we cannot change the behaviour of others, we can choose our own behaviour and do what we can to influence others in such a way that everyone is happier. The important thing at this point is just to register the reality of how we feel about the relationships that mean most to us and to assess how they add to or take away from our happiness.

Driven wild by noise

Have you ever found yourself being driven mad by the noise of other people encroaching on your space and your thoughts? It can be chatter, conflict, raised voices in the home or the office. It can be the intrusive hum of air conditioning, drone of traffic noise, the constant or the tinny second hand sound of someone else's iPod. How about the people chatting away on their mobile phones, particularly in the quiet coaches on the train? What about the loud conversations of others on the tube? Noisy neighbours can ruin your pleasure at weekends – the DIY fiends, the hedge-cutting menaces, the lawn-mowing fanatics, the intrusive noise of someone's rap music or TV programme at top volume? All of these can intrude and affect how you feel. The unwelcome noise of others can spoil a happy moment and annoy out of all proportion.

Trapped in silence

Sometimes it's the lack of communication or the silence in our environment that affects relationships. This can include feeling unable to express what you want or need or being reluctant to confront difficult issues.

> ## Susan
>
> Susan is a mother of two young children. She used to work full time as a nurse and now lives in the country – three miles from the nearest village of any sise. Her husband is in sales. He works long hours and regularly spends time away from home. Susan is lonely. She misses the companionship of her work colleagues and the fun and banter they used to have when she worked. The daily conversation with a two-year-old and a three-year-old somehow don't quite fit the bill!
>
> Susan has made one or two friends in the area, but their children are all at school and she does not see them regularly. When her husband is at home, he prefers to relax in front of the television or to read a book in what he sees as companionable silence after a day talking to clients. This change in situation has resulted in Susan becoming a much more serious person. She feels she has lost her sense of fun and much of her confidence. She has not been able to tell her husband how she feels, so her relationship with him has begun to show signs of strain and she feels they are growing apart.

Use comparisons wisely

Comparisons don't always enhance your happiness. Many people have developed the habit of looking around and comparing themselves unfavourably with others. Do you do this? They see the people they mix with as being richer, more intelligent, or better than they are in some way. If you compare yourself with someone who is a brilliant cook you might feel inferior – or alternatively, you could choose to increase your happiness by seeing them as a source of inspiration! Alternatively, why not compare yourself to others who are less talented or have less than you do?

HAPPY THOUGHT
Happiness is a choice!

Surroundings and health

Poor health can sometimes result from things that stress us in our environment. Now the odd thing is that what's good in the environment for some people may not be good for others. Let's begin however by looking at how Surroundings can have a huge impact on your health.

Give yourself a break

Changing your Surroundings can often make you feel better if you are overwhelmed, if you are jaded or if you need to look at things differently.

> ### Ben
> Ben was a student at university. Although slightly dyslexic he would not take advantage of any of the extra support or tuition that his dyslexia merited. Studying was hard and Ben worked harder and longer than most of his fellow students, just to keep up. When the exams approached, Ben studied in his room night and day but felt he was getting nowhere. The more he studied, the less he seemed to take in and the more exhausted he got... He would not take breaks because he felt he needed all the study time there was. He began to feel down and stressed. He considered giving up his university course. Then he came across an article that said how important it was for students to give themselves study breaks, to change their environment regularly and to take exercise in order to keep their physical energy high. He

started taking fresh air breaks; he went regularly to the nearby gym to exercise and sometimes just went for short walks.

The exercise and the changes in Surroundings combined, made Ben feel better and although the studying was still hard, he felt better in himself and happier. He finished his degree successfully.

HAPPY THOUGHT

To develop the Happiness Habit, focus your energy on what you can do rather than what you can't.

Surroundings and money

Money is a recurring theme in this book. On this Step of the Stairway of Happiness, its potential impact on your Surroundings is potentially enormous. It can affect the size and type of place you can live in, the location of where you live, the possessions you have, the people you meet and therefore the relationships you have, the amount of travelling you can do and the sort of hobbies you can afford. Money can also indirectly affect your health and some of the medical treatments you can access. Interestingly your Surroundings can also affect the amount of money you can earn. If you have poor health you may not be able to work. The country or location you live in may affect the amount and type of opportunities there are to earn money.

Much research has gone into the connection between money and happiness. The GDP (Gross Domestic Product) is routinely used as shorthand for the well-being of a nation. In the early stages of a climb out of poverty – either for a household or for a nation – there is a link between income and happiness. After a certain threshold, however, happiness does not keep up. People in Latin American countries for example are far happier than they should be given their economic situation.

The recurring conclusion is that money alone cannot bring happiness.

King Jigme Singye Wangchuck

The king of the small Himalayan kingdom of Bhutan, His Royal Highness King Jigme Singye Wangchuck, was concerned about the problems afflicting other developing countries that focused only on economic growth. He has therefore made *Happiness* his nation's number one priority and has introduced the GNH (Gross National Happiness) strategy.

The king believes that prosperity should be shared across Bhutan society and that it should be balanced against preserving cultural traditions and protecting the environment. The Bhutan government is now actively engaged in promoting a variety of initiatives aimed at creating the conditions most likely to improve quality of life in the most equitable way. They do not wish to see relative wealth becoming more important than quality of life

---

Brilliant Ideas to develop the Happiness Habit in your Surroundings - It will only take you 21 days!

1 List what you love

Make a list of what you love about your house, your garden and the place where you work. Include in this the country, the region, the town, the neighbourhood where you are. Take the time to pause for a moment and think how much the things you love about your Surroundings contribute to your long-term enduring happiness. Develop the Happiness Habit of focusing on what you like and love rather than what bothers you about your Surroundings.

2 Consider what you can change about your Surroundings

Make a note of the things around you that really bug you and take away from your sense of well-being and happiness. Begin to consider the possibilities for change. You may feel that many of them are outside your control and you just can't change them. What we are asking you to do is to consider what would happen if you could change them – and what will happen if you don't? The changes you decide to make do not have to be huge. Small changes can make a big difference. Planting a window box for the spring is relatively easy and inexpensive, bringing pleasure in its wake. Moving house or moving jobs is a significant step to take, often requiring courage, determination and hard work. What you have to do is work out just what a difference it would make to your life.

3 Clear the clutter

All right, let's talk about clutter. Have a look around and see all of those things you own. Go on be honest – do you need them all? How many possessions have you accumulated, thinking that one day you might need them or they could come in handy? Think about your attic, your garden shed and your garage. What treasures are lurking inside, unused, unloved and waiting for a new home. What about all those CDs, DVDs and books that you will never watch or read again? What about all those clothes, shoes, jewellery and ornaments that you don't want or wear anymore? What about that lovely jumper that Aunt Agatha gave you for your birthday that you wouldn't be seen dead in? Have a real rummage in all your cupboards and horrify yourself with what you are hoarding. Now is the time to get out the bin bags and go

to the Oxfam shop. You could even make some money on eBay®
or in car boot sales.

Feng Shui suggests that a cluttered environment means a
cluttered mind. Free your space and free your brain for happier
thoughts.

4 Start with what's easy

If you want to change something, start with something that is
easy to do and which is important to you. Take action straight
away and get the ball rolling. This will make you feel good, and
give you some energy and momentum to tackle larger issues or
projects.

Here are some suggestions on how to change your Surroundings:

- ❖ buy a plant
- ❖ wash your windows to let in more light
- ❖ weed your garden
- ❖ rearrange your furniture
- ❖ wash the paintwork
- ❖ change the lighting
- ❖ paint your room in a lighter colour
- ❖ buy a print or a picture and hang it up
- ❖ put your favourite photo in a frame on the window sill
- ❖ buy some pot pourri
- ❖ buy a bunch of flowers
- ❖ get out and about more to different pleasant environments
- ❖ visit an art gallery or a park or a stately home or a mu-
  seum
- ❖ shop in a different place
- ❖ look at your routines and work out what you can change
- ❖ change your radio station and listen to different things

❖ notice what makes you feel happy and content in your environment and be creative in finding ways of having more of those things around you.

5 Consider the impossible

Look down your list of what you want to change and look at the list of what seems impossible. For each one ask the question – What if this was possible? The impossible then becomes possible and you can consider how, if you really wanted to, this could be done, if you wanted it enough. For example, you might think that changing from an unhappy job is impossible because of family, financial or other constraints. However, it may be worth exploring what you would gain as well as lose before rejecting this as a possibility. So stop yourself from saying things such as, 'Well, I can't change that' and change it to 'If I could change that, what would it be like?'

6 Create a Happiness Album

As you go through each day, consciously register when you are happy and take a mental note of that event. At the end of the day write them down in a notebook. You now have a log of memories that will make you feel good. By constantly asking yourself the question about your current state of happiness, you are putting yourself in the driving seat and you are making the first important Step in taking charge of your overall happiness, now and in the future

If your day is one that you would rather forget, make sure you face up to and acknowledge the bad feelings caused. Once you have done that, feel free to place these memories, these events and these feelings into a place in your mind. This could be a mental filing cabinet, bonfire, locked chest, rubbish bin, post box, the bottom of the sea, sealed envelope, a star – whatever will work best for you. You are only limited by your imagination. (We

48

know one person who has a mental toy box that she puts her frustrations into and it works brilliantly for her!)

7 Peace and quiet

How much at home are you in your home? How much are you able to relax completely? Is your home a haven? Is it a place where you can relax and recharge your batteries? If it isn't, work out where it is going wrong? Is it the décor, is it the lighting, is it the temperature, is it the furniture? Is it somewhere you bring your friends and feel proud? Identify any problem area and resolve to change it.

8 Green fingers

Read the gardening tips in the weekend paper and decide to carry some of them out. Plant out pots for spring and pots for autumn.

9 Time for you

Give yourself a bit of space. Resolve that however busy you might need to be, make time for yourself and do something for you that is a treat. It could be reading a chapter of a book, a long bath, a long telephone call with a friend, taking 30 minutes out for lunch rather than eating on the run, deciding to go and watch your local football team, stopping to chat with a colleague or friend even when you are in a rush, listening to a favourite radio programme, or having a takeaway instead of cooking a meal.

10 Now is the time

Ensure that you value the pleasure of the here and now rather than putting all of your energies into the past or the future. Stop yourself from time to time and simply be conscious of the good things that are going on for you at the moment. Try saying something positive to yourself such as, 'I'm happy about ...' or 'I'm really lucky to have/to be ...'.

11 Weigh it all up

Look at the balance in every area of your life. For example, if work were taken away, what would you have left? If you retired tomorrow or won the lottery, what would you do? When we say work we mean the full range from high powered, high paid jobs to managing a home and children or doing unpaid volunteer work. Are you sure you have managed the balance of activities and interests in your life? What would you do with your time if you did not work?

12 Thank you for the music

Have you got enough music in your life? It can certainly change your mood. Some tunes and songs change your mood instantly and bring happy memories flooding back. One song can transport you to the wonderful holiday, the perfect relationship, the great night out or anytime when you were in a situation where you were happy. A brilliant way to bring about a vast improvement in your mood would be to remember those songs and replay them. Listening to the music will allow you to focus on those happy feelings you enjoyed at that time and to make them part of your current life.

Equally, music can bring back sad or unhappy times. If your favourite tune is played at a funeral, a party where you had a row, were in hospital or on a holiday where you didn't enjoy yourself, it will evoke unhappy memories and bring past feelings into the present. A clever way therefore to protect yourself from unnecessary feelings of unease or sadness is to steer clear of music with the wrong associations. Only tap into happy memories!

13 Concentrate

When worries absorb your daily thoughts, doing something else that requires total concentration can mean that you forget your problems for a brief time. Why not learn to play a musical instrument or join a choir, a group, a band, or have fun with any kind of musical activity that makes you feel good. Go to a concert, a live theatre production and see just how invigorating it is. Why not join a squash club, do Sudoku, become a crossword fiend, learn to play Chess or take up any activity that needs focus and provides you with energy and the feel-good factor.

Equally, if you usually spend time rushing around worrying about your own life, not watching television, try spending an evening in. Find a programme that interests you and immerse yourself in it.

14 The happy office

Look at your office with fresh eyes. Do you like the room, the office where you work? Look at it objectively and see it as it really is. Look at the décor, the state of the carpet, the pictures on the walls and the piles of paper that surround you. Do you have a tidy environment or are you working round piles of things you could file away? Have you got plants, flowers, photographs or do you sidestep dirty coffee cups, old newspapers and letters, printouts of e-mails that you will never look at again. Get out a bin liner and throw things out. Move your furniture around. Buy a plant. Give yourself a fresh, orderly office and you will find that new ideas will come from a new perspective.

16 The leisure bubble

There are a number of ways in which sport and hobbies can create a land of bubbles where you can 'lose' yourself and be truly in the moment. Athletes call this being in 'the zone' but it also applies to many other activities. Being in the zone means that the anxieties, stresses, frustrations of modern life and living seem to melt away. Being in a leisure bubble is like taking a mini holiday. Here are some ways to create a leisure bubble.

❖ Choose an exercise activity you enjoy such as jogging, working out, swimming, walking, yoga, Pilates, t'ai chi, dancing, martial arts, gardening, etc. and do it regularly.

❖ Visit some art galleries, museums or exhibitions. Take time to study what you see, making no judgements, but simply register the experience. Once good way to do this is to defocus your eyes while looking at (say) a painting or sculpture. It's as if you are looking at and through the object at the same time. This puts you into a trance-like state which enhances the experience and keeps you in the moment.

17 Escape the trap

If you are trapped in your Surroundings, check first of all whether this is truly something you can't change. Say to yourself, 'There is always a choice' and then consider what the choices are. You may not like the choices in front of you, but that does not mean that there is no choice. If you genuinely can't see any, then say to yourself, 'If there was a choice what would it be?' and pay attention to the first answer that springs to mind.

WORK BOOK

Workbook Step 1 – Surroundings

Guide to using the Workbook

When you are going through this Workbook, you will find some of the questions easier than others. Sometimes the answers will spring instantly to mind. Other times you may need to take time out to reflect and consider what this could mean for you.

You may find it useful to go through a checklist of the areas that could affect your happiness. When answering these questions, some of the things you think about with regard to your Surroundings could be:

❖ the relationships that surround you
❖ the effect of money on your surroundings
❖ what your work environment is like
❖ your physical health and well-being and that of those close to you.

This is about how you look at your Surroundings and how they affect your happiness.

    A What are the **three** things in your physical Surroundings that make you happiest? E.g. your garden, your car, your iPod, your view from your window, birds singing, a photograph, a child's drawing on the fridge door, being in the town, being in the country…

1   ....

    ....

2 ....

....

3 ....

....

B What are the three things in your Surroundings which, if you changed them, would add most to your happiness?

1 ....

....

2 ....

....

3 ....

....

C What are the three things in your Surroundings that, if you changed them, could decrease your unhappiness?

1 ....

....

2 ....

....

3   ....
    ....
    ....

D What **one** thing could somebody else do for you, if you
   asked them, that would increase your happiness?

   ....
   ....
   ....

E What **one** thing could somebody else do, if you asked
   them, that could decrease your unhappiness?

   ....
   ....
   ....

The Happiness Challenge for Step 1 on the
Stairway of Happiness - Surroundings

THE HAPPINESS MANTRA

Your happiness state will only change if you do things differently and if you increase the number of Happiness Habits you
develop. Remember it takes only 21 days to create permanent
change

In order to increase your happiness, take the Happiness Challenge.
Take one of the actions that you have identified in this Workbook.
Every day for 21 days, stop just thinking about making this change.
Go out and do it!

Think hard about what you have written above. Decide now what actions you will take to increase the happiness you can gain from your Surroundings. Make sure you write them down.

Actions:

....

....

....

New habit to be developed

....

....

....

Keep a check on your progress. Put a tick in the box every day for 21 days when you have practised that habit.

Progress Chart						
Day 1	Day 2	Day 3	Day 4	Day 5	Day 6	Day 7
Day 8	Day 9	Day 10	Day 11	Day 12	Day 13	Day 14
Day 15	Day 16	Day 17	Day 18	Day 19	Day 20	Day 21

Start date ....

4

Behaviour

The Second Step on the Stairway of Happiness

This is the second Step towards the goal of ultimate happiness, the place where we examine what it is that we are doing in our everyday lives and how it affects our happiness. Now is our chance to explore ways in which we can change what we do to improve our situation and how happy we are. So as you go through this chapter, keep asking yourself the question, 'Do the things I do and the way I behave increase or decrease the amount of happiness in my life?'

Remember! To make lasting changes to what you don't like about the things you do and the unhelpful habits you've got into, you may need to work at one Step above on the Stairway of Happiness. In other words, you need to check that you have the Skills and Capabilities to change those aspects of your Behaviour that you are unhappy with.

Step 6 – Purpose
Purpose is what brings meaning into your life. It's why you are here.

Step 5 – Identity
Identity is about acknowledging your roots and accepting yourself for who you are.

Step 4 – Values and Beliefs
Values and Beliefs are the programming, power, motivation and energy behind your actions.

Step 3 – Skills and Capabilities
Skills and Capabilities are all the talents you have or could have, given the opportunity.

Step 2 – Behaviour
Behaviour includes what you do, how you do it, who you do it with and how others behave with you. It's also about what you think, what you say and how you say it.

Step 1 – Surroundings
Your Surroundings are everything you see, hear and feel when you look around you. It's your environment and the results you are getting.

Behaviour

What we mean by Behaviour includes what you do, how you do it, who you do it with and how others behave with you. It's also about what you think, what you say and how you say it. It's about the recognition that what you do and say have an impact on how happy you feel. This is not only what you say out loud to others but it's your internal voice whispering in your ear. Behaviour is about choice. It's about taking responsibility for your own actions and the way you respond to the situations that you have to deal with every day in life. This includes your attitude and your emo-

> tional responses. It's whether you tap into your good memories or focus on the bad things that have happened in the past

Look around you. How can you be happy …

- ❖ if you are not able to do the things you want to do
- ❖ if you go around upsetting others by the things you say
- ❖ if you are continually blaming others for your misfortunes
- ❖ if you dwell on the negative and unhappy things in life
- ❖ if you can't help eating, drinking or overspending too much
- ❖ if you mentally beat yourself up when you do something wrong or stupid
- ❖ if you act before you think
- ❖ if you depend on others to make you happy?

The starting point on the second Step of happiness is that we are all responsible for our behaviours. This means that you are more in control of what happens to you than you think. Because you are in control of your actions and your actions are not in control of you, you own the consequences of all your behaviours. What you choose to do or choose not to do will impact directly on your state of happiness.

You are 100% responsible for what you do.

Career crossroads

Peter had worked for a high street retailer selling electronic goods and had been doing it since he left school three years ago. Although he loved the products and was a natural salesman, he felt he was getting nowhere despite getting his NVQ qualifications. He therefore applied for a job at a local sports centre as a trainee manager and got it at a similar salary. When he resigned, his manager asked him why he had not discussed it with him before. The manager said that if only he had known how unsettled Peter was, he could have got him on a training scheme. However, it was too late. As a result, the manager felt betrayed by someone he thought was a loyal employee and Peter was left wondering if he had made the right decision.

Looking at it from the outside we can see that if Peter had handled this differently, he could have given himself a real choice about his career. He could have found an opportunity to talk to the manager and express his concerns about his career direction. Equally the manager could have had regular informal sessions with his team to gauge how they were feeling about their work. Communication had failed them all round and therefore had a direct impact on each of them.

Personal power

If you are feeling good about life and if you tend to recall positive, happy memories, then you are more inclined to act in a more confident and positive manner. However, if your natural tendency is to recall difficult times and unhappy memories, then you will be more hesitant, readier to take a darker view of the situation and more likely to invite unhappiness into your life. Although you cannot control what happens to you in your life, you can control how you react to it. Accepting responsibility for the state of your happiness at the moment and deciding to adopt Happiness Habits puts control of life squarely with you. This is true personal power.

Assume therefore that where you are in your life now is a direct result of all the behaviours in your life up to this very moment. In other words you are the direct result of everything you have said, thought and done (or not said, thought and done!) up to now. This means that the state of your relationships, the job you are in, the state of your finances, the home that you have – all of these are a result of actions in the past. If you are not where you want to be at this moment, then now is the time to change those behaviours that have brought you to where you are. If you keep on doing the same thing you will get the same result so change your behaviour and see the instant impact on your happiness. Think carefully as you use this wonderful new personal power and be ready for all the exciting new changes it will bring to your life.

The Shanghai expatriate business men with their Worldmark ringleaders did not realise the power that they had. They thought they were relaxing and enjoying themselves but they were planting the seeds of change to bring happiness into the lives of orphans.

A Happy Story from China

Every day after work a group of guys all working in Suzhou, China, met at Blue Marlin 3 to relax with a beer after what they like to describe as a hard day's toil. These people have in common the fact that they are working for international businesses, developing manufacturing and sales for their organisations. They also share a liking for beer, relaxation and laughter.

At the end of the evening when the bill was called for, it was always rounded up and the left-over amount put into what the founding members of the after-work club – Mickey Duff, Jim Bews, Keith (Mr Whiskey Jack) Cairncross, Phil Murray and Jim Bell – called 'The Happy Fund'. Their plan was always that The Happy Fund would subsidise a night out. Then they discovered that they had more in common than they thought – a deeply caring and charitable streak – so they decided that their Happy Fund would be given to an orphanage in Suzhou.

They discovered that two children needed heart surgery, one little one had spina bifida and two little girls needed cleft pallet operations. Since May 2004 five children have had major surgery paid directly from The Happy Fund. All of the Blue Marlin 3 after-work drinkers e-mailed their friends and money flowed into The Happy Fund. John and Elaine Dargan got married and asked for Happy contributions instead. Rod McMillan, not renowned for his physical prowess, did a road race through Edinburgh and raised thousands for them.

The Happy Fund grew and grew and continues to grow. There are no administrative costs, no bank charges, just money going directly for hospital costs and operations for orphans. The Suzhou Volunteer Group works with the children, identifying those who need help and making sure they get it. Teresa Bratton, a devoted and caring lady, sends out e-mails to let the Happy Funders know what is happening so we all rejoice to hear of the recovery of one, just as we mourn when one is lost.

Teresa and her friends actively help and support the orphanage. They visit every day to help care for the children. They manage the money, they pay the doctors directly, they fight their way through the bureaucracy and make sure that the children benefit directly from every single penny.

There is talk of building a school so that the orphans will have an education and therefore a better start in life. There is other talk of diversifications to use the fund to help in other ways. The original target was to raise RMB 80 000 which they did in remarkably short order. The amount raised since inception is now close to RMB 300 000.

At the Blue Marlin 3 they continue to drink their beer after work. The change still goes to The Happy Fund and life-saving operations are the result. Now that's what I call a fund of happiness!

> If you would like your loose change to alter a child's life, e-mail us at anne@switchtosuccess.co.uk and we will let you know how to be a member of the world's happiest drinking club.

The internal voice

Inside our head we each have a voice that talks to us, giving a running commentary as we go through life. The best kind of voice to have that will be a mentor along the road to happiness is the friendly, kind supportive voice that tells you how good you are, how you are bound to pass the exam, how you are sure to catch the train, how it is clear that the new boss likes you, that the task you have been set is an easy one for you. Usually, however, this little voice taps into our self-doubt, however deep rooted it may be and however deep we think we may have hidden it. It likes to say things such as, 'You are bound to be late', 'You will never manage that', ' I can tell he hates you', 'This is just too hard for you', 'You shouldn't have worn that dress', 'You are really out of your depth with this one'.

The little voice does a very powerful job in undermining your self-belief and self-confidence, causing you to question your self-worth, your relationships with others and how other people see you. Learning how to quell it and to change it into the supportive voice we each need will inevitably lead to more success and more happiness.

What you secretly believe about yourself and what you say to yourself can also impact on your health. A sure way to feel ill and to increase anxiety about your health is to go onto the internet and look up any of your small ailments. Within five minutes you will know that you are heading for a heart attack or have contracted a rare form of some fatal disease. On the other hand, if you stay away from thoughts of illness and focus instead on health and healthy thoughts, then you will be training your mind to recognise that it lives in a healthy body.

> ## Healthy living
>
> Linda was one of three children in a family where everyone suffered from poor health. She got into the habit of telling other people she was not a healthy person. She repeated what her mother used to say frequently when she was a small child, 'We are a poorly family.' Linda became a health practitioner, but still suffered from poor health into her early 40s. One day she woke up to the fact that she was acting like someone who expected to be ill and her body obliged and that she didn't actually believe that this was true. She changed what she said to herself and others. She assumed she was a healthy person and from that moment on many of her minor and chronic ailments vanished and her life and happiness both changed dramatically for the better.

The power of 21st-century communication

Good relationships grow out of clear and positive communication. The opportunities in the 21st century to cloud the channels of communication are greater than they ever were. We can get in touch instantly by text, telephone or e-mail rather than the more thoughtful processes that were relied on before the advent of mobile telephones and computers. Getting in touch with people used to be by a letter that would take time to write and then to post. In the course of that letter writing, words could be changed or sentences crossed out. A letter written in the heat of the moment used to sit on the hall table or on the mantelpiece so that there was time to think again, rewrite it and communicate in a different way. Now a text arrives and is responded to in a flash. Offence can be taken in a split second when no offence was meant. E-mails fly in and out via broadband and cross the world in a split second. Anything put together in a moment of anger or fear or homesickness or guilt will be gone and cannot be retrieved. There is no place for second thoughts in the world of 21st-century communication and this can have a dire impact on relationships. Being at odds with colleagues, friends and family casts an instant shadow on happiness and it can take a long time to shake it off.

What are you doing now that is contributing to your future happiness?

Sacked over a ham sandwich

Two secretaries at one of Sydney's top law firms were sacked after an e-mail exchange was circulated around the city's legal district.

The fight began over a missing ham sandwich and finished with one secretary taunting the other for being unable to hold on to a boyfriend.

The e-mail exchange began when one secretary sent a group e-mail to colleagues in the firm's Sydney head office asking if anyone had stolen her lunch. She wrote, 'Yesterday I put my lunch in the fridge on level 19 which included a packet of ham, some cheese slices and two slices of bread which was going to be for my lunch today. Overnight it has gone missing and as I have no spare money to buy another lunch today, I would appreciate being reimbursed for it.'

Another secretary replied suggesting that she had probably left her lunch on a different floor. The e-mail exchange then went rapidly downhill with one taunting the other for being blonde. The other replied, 'Being a brunette doesn't mean you're smart, though.' The e-mail reply was to the point, calling her 'Miss Can't Keep A Boyfriend'.

As all of the office was being copied into this heated exchange, it wasn't long before the e-mails were sweeping Sydney's offices, delighting all who read it. A company spokesman said anyone involved in passing on the e-mail would be disciplined. 'E-mail is a business tool, not a personal messaging system – the use of it in this case was not in any way acceptable, nor is that the way we expect people to treat their work colleagues,' he said.

The spokesman said he still did not know whether or not Ms Nugent's lunch was stolen.

Happiness lies within

The starting point for happiness has to come from within. It does not lie in anyone else's power to make you happy. Someone may be able to take you to the places you want to go, accompany you on the path you want to follow but no one can affect how you feel inside. Perhaps this is the reason why one marriage in three ends in divorce. Marriage is rarely the fairy tale we dream about but requires consistent effort, energy and flexibility to build the lasting relationship most of us are seeking. Disappointment can lead to recriminations and a deep-seated unhappiness in core relationships.

Recognise the power of your filters

Remember how it is when you meet someone who intrigues you, captures your interest and who seems to be your kind of person? You like so many things about them, the way they talk, the way they laugh and the way that they behave. You identify interests in common, coincidences in your life to date and the fascination of overlapping lives. The filter that you are using is one that only allows the good things through. You simply don't see any of the small irritations that might well be there all along.

However, when the initial enthusiasm wanes, the filter you are using changes. Suddenly you don't see the points that unite you but only those that divide you. Your focus has changed to identifying where you clash rather than where you gel. This works for children in the playground as much as it does for couples in relationships. Happiness is built on unity and harmony whereas unhappiness is built on discord and difference.

Emotional hijacks

When relationships are running well and smoothly, we tend to relax and feel cheerful. However, when they go wrong we are upset, out of sorts and anxious. It can affect our mood, our sleep pattern, our eating habits and how we feel. It can also mean that we become irritable and behave in ways we would prefer not to. Think of the times when you have behaved in a way that is out of character for you, when you have lost your temper, shouted, cried, overreacted in an emotional way. It could be that you are quiet when you are normally talkative or reclusive when you usually are out and about with friends. That's when you have been emotionally hijacked and that is when your relationships with others are at the greatest risk. If your colleagues, customers, friends, relatives are hurt or offended or anxious about you, then the tone of your conversations will change and you will be run the risk of further misunderstandings.

What kind of future happiness are you creating by behaving the way you are behaving now?

Just in time to be too late

Are you someone who loves being on time? Are you the one who is always ready ten minutes early, at the railway station half an hour before the train departs, at the doctor's fifteen minutes before your appointment or are you the one who comes running down the station platform one minute before the train leaves, the person who is always apologising for being slightly late because the traffic was bad or the car wouldn't start? We have got news for you. The superbly organised types who run their lives by the clock, making lists, always on time and reading the map they bought a week ago are simply mystifying to those who believe that ten minutes late is arriving on time. And equally, those of you who are always running late with excellent excuses for why this is the case are driving the other ones wild. The conflict caused by this is dazzling. The organised, systematic and punctual are seen to be inflexible and blinkered by their options-driven colleagues who in turn are seen to be disorganised and rude. The truth is that everyone ends up where they want to be in life but we can all choose our preferred route and method to get there. The misunderstanding that can be caused by the difference in style can cause conflict in relationships and eat away at an otherwise happy arrangement.

The courtesy of kings

Jane was the newly appointed managing director of a company. She was enthusiastic and ambitious, full of plans for the business to get it back on a growth plan. After a couple of months in the business when she was beginning to impress her board colleagues with her strategy and her style, she came up with a stunning new idea for the business. She called a meeting for 8 AM the next day and told her co-directors that they all had to be there. Meetings were changed, plans were altered and at 7.45 the next day, they were all there – with one exception. Jane turned up half an hour late at 8.30 and chaired the meeting as though nothing had happened. She failed to see that her colleagues were seriously fed up at being kept waiting, especially as they had cancelled their plans to be there. Jane was unaware that she was late and that she had caused offence. The result was that her colleagues were now unhappy with her style, believing

> that she was arrogant and uncaring. The new ideas she had were not met with the enthusiasm they deserved and an air of unhappiness crept into the board room.

Remember that your 'on time' might be someone else's 'late'.

Brilliant Ideas to develop the Happiness Habit in your behaviour – it will only take you 21 days!

1 How to stop petty arguments and rows that seem to go on and on

Now is the time to ban from your life the unproductive, energy sapping debates that are not about something of any importance anyway. In calm moments of reflection, the most aggravating of arguments are usually about the most trivial of issues. They usually are about who lost the tickets, who should have brought the map, who put jam in the butter, whose turn it is to empty the dishwasher and who used up the last of the milk. How many times do you have the same old arguments on the same old subjects? If you find yourself arguing about who does the shopping, who's going to be the sober driver, why we are never on time for anything and which channel are we going to watch on the television, then now is the time to change.

As it takes two people to engage in any argument, then resolve to be the one who will behave differently. Don't wait for someone else to change what they say or do – you be the one to initiate change. For example if you argue about the division of housework, try this new strategy.

1   Be very clear about what you want and ask for it! Never assume that the other person knows what you want.

2   Tell them how you feel and how important it is to you to have this issue resolved.

3   Get them to commit to a specific action or actions.

4   Ask them what is important to them and make sure you accommodate this.

Apply this technique to whatever area is causing irritation and watch out for improved results!

2 Just too late to be on time

If you are someone who loves organisation, schedules, plans and knowing exactly what you are doing and when you are doing it and if you live or work with someone who operates in a different way, choose something that is relatively unimportant and this time do it in a way that you normally wouldn't. For example, if you normally book tickets for the cinema before you go, don't bother this time. All the tickets may be sold out, so you may end up watching a film you might not have chosen. By changing your behaviour, it will have an effect on the person you are with. You may find that people like the new carefree you or they may miss the organisation you previously brought to their life. Whatever it is and however you do it, the result will be an increased awareness of what your relationship is and how happy you are within it.

If you are the one who always keeps someone waiting, be the one this time who is nonchalantly swinging the car keys, bag packed and ready to go, ten minutes ahead of time. You could decide to be the one who is going to be the planner, the table booker, the list maker, the holiday organiser and watch to see how the dynamics change in your relationship. See if this makes you more happy or less happy – and adjust accordingly!

3 The elephant in the room

Have you ever felt uncomfortable in a relationship where you both find it impossible to talk about an important issue?

It could be something small, for example you invite someone to lunch and they don't turn up. The next time you see them, you feel awkward about mentioning it but you are also aggrieved, irritated and hurt. The other person doesn't mention it either and it hangs between you as an invisible obstacle that gets in the way of a happy relationship.

It could be something big. Perhaps a wife knows her husband is having an affair but she fears the consequences of challenging him. Equally he suspects that she may have found him out. Ignoring this particular elephant has led to growing estrangement and isolation within the relationship.

Check out if an elephant is the room in the relationships you have. It will take courage to acknowledge the elephant and discuss what to do. It will also bring relief and will be the first step in resolving the issue.

4 Making the most of your colleagues

Research shows that having a best friend at work is a key ingredient of happiness at work. If you have a colleague whom you trust and like, you can share successes, problems, ideas, jokes and thoughts with them, meaning that both of you will be more successful in your jobs, the team will do better and the business will benefit. Have you got a friend and an ally at work? If not, try out these ideas to track one down!

How to find a best friend at work.

- ❖ The next time you get into the lift, talk to whoever is there with you.
- ❖ Decide to use e-mail only when you have to and drop by a colleague's desk instead of phoning or e-mailing.

- ❖ Take a proper lunch break instead of having a sandwich at your desk. Find someone in the company to eat with.
- ❖ Show interest in and get to know people in another section or department. Listen to them and find ways to help them out. Then you will find that they do the same for you.
- ❖ See if you can organise an event for outside work hours. It could be a five-a-side football match, a bowling evening or a pizza night.
- ❖ If your company sponsors a particular charity, organise a fund-raising event, however small. If they don't have a charity, suggest that they do and get people on board.
- ❖ Bring a cake in to the office on your birthday and share it with colleagues.

If you are self-employed and work from home, forge links with like-minded people in the same situation. Find out about local business networks and make an effort to join. Share information and ideas and look for ways to work together. These new relationships will make you feel happier in your working life and lead to improved results.

5 Do something unexpected

A healthy and comfortable part of relationships is the reliability of how people are likely to behave. You know what people will do and people know what you will do. However, you can prevent boredom seeping in to your relationship and add sparkle to your life by changing your normal pattern of behaviour.

Why not try some of these ideas.

- ❖ Buy an unexpected present.
- ❖ Buy your supermarket shopping on line for a change and use the time you save to go out with your family for a walk.

- ❖ Switch the television off for a week and find other things to do.
- ❖ Leave the car in the garage and go out with your family on foot.
- ❖ The next time you drive past someone you know at a bus stop, offer them a lift.
- ❖ Eat together at a different time. If you usually eat in the kitchen, eat in the dining room and vice versa.

6 Do it your way

Happiness cannot be built on the back of 'should', 'could' and 'ought'. The route to personal fulfilment is choosing what is right for you. Write a list of the things you regularly say to yourself.

'I should …'
'I shouldn't …'
'I could…'
'I couldn't …'
'I must …'
'I mustn't …'.

Think through how you would be if you were to say:

'I choose to …'
'I choose not to …'
'I want to …'
'I don't want to …'
'I may …'
'I may not …'.

Doing this makes sure you are back in the driving seat of your own life, following your own path, not following a path set out by someone else.

7 Death to routine

Routine is part of our lives. Look at your own life and identify those areas of routine. Maybe your weekends always follow the same path of supermarket shopping, washing, working, cooking meals, taking children to their various activities, watching *The X Factor* and watching or playing sport and cooking Sunday lunch. Decide now which of these routines have become dull and meaningless, adding nothing to your life. If the shopping is a tedious chore, maybe you could do it on a Thursday night or do it through the internet. If watching TV on a Saturday night has become a habit, think of different ways to bring a bit of spark into your life. Replace routine with ritual – something to look forward to rather than dread. The ritual is full of the excitement of the unknown. It could take you to the cinema rather than a DVD, it could take you for long walks instead of doing the garden. It could be reading a book rather than watching TV. You could go to the local pub, you could take up salsa dancing – anything that makes a small step-change in your life.

8 Check the balance

Look at your life to decide if there are areas you overdo. Do you overeat, overwork, over-train, overdrink, overspend, over-shop, or generally just get the balance wrong? Be honest about the effect on your life. Do they add to your happiness or are they bad habits? Ask yourself, 'Why am I doing this? Is this a Happiness Habit?' Are you over-extending in different ways in order to compensate for areas you are avoiding?

9 The right job for you

Take time to think about the job that you have and decide if it is making you happy now, and if it is likely to lead to happiness in the future. Think about your personal development – are you learning new skills and adding to your skill set? Can you see the next step up the career ladder or the next increase in salary? If you are happy doing your job today, do you think you will be just as happy in three years time?

Look over the parapet and look at what other jobs you could do. Look at the job advertisements in the national, local or trade press. The next time you are on the internet have a look at a recruitment website. Compare your current job with what is on offer and see if you could improve your lot. Try applying for a job and use the selection process to see what you could be getting elsewhere.

10 The commuter

Are you sick of the daily commute? How long does it take you to get to work every day? Maybe what seemed like a reasonable commuting distance a couple of years ago has become a longer journey because of increased volume of traffic. Count up the time each day that you spend travelling to work, then multiply it by 5 and then multiply it by 46. You will then have the amount of time in a year that you spend going to and from work.

Some people love that time in the car, adjusting from home to work and work to home. Others don't. If you would like to reclaim some of that for your personal life, think about different ways of doing so. You could work at home for one day a week, you could move house so you are nearer work or you could decide to find a job nearer home. You could car-share with someone so that you have company on the way. You could use travelling time for reading or listening to audio books or for listening to your favourite music.

11 Earning more

Are you being paid enough? Everyone can find a use for more money, whether it is to move to a bigger house, improve the one you have, buy furniture you need, get a better car or just money to help you pay the bills. Look at what you are earning and decide whether you are getting what you deserve. Think about what added value you could give at work. What would happen if you made a few extra telephone calls, sent out a couple more letters, improved the database, initiated an idea? Could you do something that would make a difference at work, get yourself noticed and mark you out for an increase in salary, a bigger bonus or a promotion? The more you put in, the more you will take out. Put your energy into improving your performance at work. Go beyond the expected and get back more than you expect.

12 A little extra

How about getting a little extra cash? When you look around you at home in the cupboards, wardrobes, garage and shed, be ruthless when sorting things out. Look at all those things you will never use again. Get them all together and take them all to the car boot sale on Sunday. Turn it into a day out for the family so you win a tidier environment, a happy family event and a sum of money you otherwise wouldn't have.

13 Counting sheep

Tiredness makes us more vulnerable and less able to cope or see the positives when life is not running smoothly. It's harder to keep your sense of humour and to feel happy when you are tired than it is when you are bounding around full of energy. Many people suffer from sleeping problems, so here are some tips that will help you get a good night's sleep and give you energy.

❖ Treat your bedroom as a haven. Have fresh flowers, fresh air, relaxing or inspiring pictures or photos. Don't work in your bedroom as it can be more difficult to sleep in a room you work in.

❖ Have more exercise during the day. This helps burn up adrenaline build-up in the brain which results in nervous tension.

❖ Have a regular sleeping pattern with set bed-times and wake-up times for at least three days. This will give your body clock a frame of reference and expectation about sleeping.

❖ Drink herbal/decaffeinated drinks rather than alcohol, tea or coffee before going to bed. Milky drinks are also good as milk contains tryptophan – a substance that helps to produce a relaxed state of mind.

❖ Try a passionflower tranquiliser. It's one of the best natural sleep remedies and is non-habit forming.

❖ If you can't get to sleep because your mind is busy, then notice each thought as it comes to you. Let it float away or mentally file it away so that your brain can deal with it while you sleep. Knowing that all your problems and thoughts will be processed well while you sleep will allow your conscious mind to rest and make it easier for sleep to come.

14 Behave as if you were a lucky person

Some people see themselves as naturally lucky individuals and have assumed the behaviour of lucky people. They act as if life is going to go their way and have the conscious behaviours of lucky people. Lucky people are generally happy people, so why not choose to be lucky? There are seven principles of luck that you can adopt in order to increase your happiness.

Research has proved the following.

❖ Lucky people are in control of their response to the events and situations that happen to them.
Tip: Accept you are the master of your destiny and that you are not a victim.

❖ Lucky people finish off what they start and have the tenacity and perseverance to see things through, even when the odds are against them.
Tip: Keep going to achieve the things that no one, not even you, thought possible.

❖ Lucky people have the confidence to take a chance rather than plumping for the safe bet. They have a willingness to think differently and keep an open mind
Tip: Do something different and take a chance where normally your natural caution might hold you back and deprive you of a chance to find happiness in a different way.

❖ Lucky people use all their senses and intuition to heighten awareness about possible lucky opportunities.
Tip: Remember that you have an 'inner voice' that will help you find the road to happiness. Listen to it and see what a difference it will make.

❖ Lucky people have the ability to get on well with lots of people in many different contexts.
Tip: Concentrate on what you have in common with everyone you meet rather than what divides you and see the benefits it will bring.

❖ Lucky people have an optimistic outlook and know how to shrug off worries and concerns.
Tip: Be determined to see the positives in all situations. Focus on the positive and not the negative and turn this into a habit.

❖ Lucky people know themselves well enough to know what works well for them and what can work against them.

Tip: Use all of your skills and resources to make sure you create happiness in all that you do.

Visit www.switchtosuccess.co.uk and do the Luck questionnaire. Use the feedback report that you will receive to decide what you need to do to improve your luck and therefore your happiness.

15 Keeping busy

If you are consciously happy, then activity seems to flow naturally. You don't have to think about what you want to do as you are cheerful, happy and enjoying life. However, if life is difficult and you are going through a bad patch, a good way to keep unhappiness at bay is to plan things to do. While you are engaged in purposeful activity, it will be hard for the unhappy thoughts to get through. If you are feeling low at the moment, think about what you can do. We don't mean big events like planning to move house or booking a major holiday. It is small things that you can look forward to and enjoy 'in the moment'.

Look at the list below and decide if any of them would cheer you up. Add your own ideas to the list.

- ❖ Treat yourself to a magazine you don't normally read.
- ❖ Meet a friend for a coffee.
- ❖ Telephone a friend and have a chat.
- ❖ Send a letter to someone you haven't been in touch with for a while.
- ❖ Catch a train to a place nearby that you haven't visited in ages.
- ❖ Cook a special meal.
- ❖ Bake a cake.
- ❖ Fix something in the house that has been irritating you.
- ❖ Move the furniture round.
- ❖ Buy a bunch of flowers or a plant.
- ❖ Go to the cinema.

- ❖ Go for a walk.
- ❖ Do something that breaks the routine.

16 The secret formula for happiness

There is a secret formula for happiness. In order to benefit from it you need to do an exercise first. Here it is.

1 Choose a lovely memory from the past. It should be one that makes you feel instantly happy or feel instantly good when you think of it.

2 Go inside (it sometimes helps if you close your eyes) and relive the experience. See what you saw, hear what you hear and feel what you felt. This should feel really good.

3 Play it as a movie in your mind's eye and make a note of exactly what you see.

Now for the good part. What exactly did you see?

(a) Dissociated

When you replay the movie, do you see the whole of yourself in the picture – rather as if you are watching a movie with yourself as the lead role?

OR

(b) Associated

Are you actually inside the movie, looking through your own eyes and seeing what you saw at the time?

Now replay the movie. If you were Associated the first time, visualise the scene as if you are Dissociated. What happens? There is less of an emotional charge. On the other hand, if your picture was Dissociated the first time, try Associating with it. You will feel more emotion.

If you find this hard to do, just practise a few times and it will become easier.

So here's the secret formula for happiness.

- ❖ Dissociate from the bad memories of life. They will bother you less.
- ❖ Associate into the good memories. You will have more good feelings. Every time you need to feel happier, simply associate into a good memory from the past and you will feel happy instantly.

WORK BOOK

Workbook Step 2 - Behaviour

Guide to using the Workbook

When you are going through this workbook, you will find some of the questions easier than others. Sometimes the answers will spring instantly to mind. Other times you may need to take time out to reflect and consider what this could mean for you.

You may find it useful to go through a checklist of the areas that could affect your happiness. When answering these questions, some of the things you think about with regard to your Behaviour could be:

* the way you handle your relationships
* your attitude and approach to money
* how your behaviour in your work environment affects your happiness
* what you do that affects your physical health and well being and that of those close to you.

This is about looking at the things that you do and seeing how they affect your happiness.

> A What are the **three** things that you do that you love doing most and make you feel good?
>
> 1 ....
>   ....
>   ....

2 ....
....
....
3 ....
....
....

B What are the **three** things that you feel you have to do, that you dislike most?

1 ....
....
....
2 ....
....
....
3 ....
....
....

C What **three** things do you do that, if you stopped doing them, would make you feel great?

1 ....
....
....
2 ....
....
....
3 ....
....
....

D What **one** thing could somebody else stop doing that would increase your happiness?

....
....

....

E What **one** thing could somebody else stop doing that
   could decrease your unhappiness?

....

....

....

Think hard about what you have written above. Decide now
what new Behaviours you will adopt that are most likely to add
to your happiness. Make sure you write them down.

Actions:

....

....

....

The Happiness Challenge for Step 2 on the
Stairway of Happiness - Behaviour

THE HAPPINESS MANTRA
Your happiness state will only change if you do things differently and if you increase the number of Happiness Habits you
develop. Remember it takes only 21 days to create permanent
change.

In order to increase your happiness, take the Happiness Challenge.
Take one of the actions that you have identified in this Workbook.
Every day for 21 days, stop just thinking about making this change.
Go out and do it!

New habit to be developed

....

....

....

Keep a check on your progress. Put a tick in the box every day for 21 days when you have practised that habit.

Progress Chart						
Day 1	Day 2	Day 3	Day 4	Day 5	Day 6	Day 7
Day 8	Day 9	Day 10	Day 11	Day 12	Day 13	Day 14
Day 15	Day 16	Day 17	Day 18	Day 19	Day 20	Day 21

Start date ....

5

Skills and Capabilities

You have now worked through the Steps of Surroundings and Behaviour and now is the time to examine the talents you have and what you are doing with them. Are you making the most of all your talents and gifts? How happy are you with your progress so far?

Remember! To make lasting changes to the Skills and Capabilities that are not giving you the results you want, you may need to work at least one Step above on the Stairway of Happiness. In other words, you may need to change some of the Values and Beliefs that are not working for you, reassess your Identity or clarify your Purpose.

Step 6 – Purpose
Purpose is what brings meaning into your life. It's why you are here.

Step 5 – Identity
Identity is about acknowledging your roots and accepting yourself for who you are.

Step 4 – Values and Beliefs
Values and Beliefs are the programming, power, motivation and energy behind your actions.

Step 3 – Skills and Capabilities
Skills and Capabilities are all the talents you have or could have, given the opportunity.

Step 2 – Behaviour
Behaviour includes what you do, how you do it, who you do it with and how others behave with you. It's also about what you think, what you say and how you say it.

Step 1 – Surroundings
Your Surroundings are everything you see, hear and feel when you look around you. It's your environment and the results you are getting.

Skills and Capabilities

Skills and Capabilities cover a very wide range. This is not just about examination success, formal qualifications or certificates, badges or medals that prove your worth. It includes a huge range of skills which you are capable of growing if you put your mind to it or if you have the opportunity. Some skills come naturally and others need working at. It encompasses how you manage your physical well-being and health ensuring you are in the best possible state to make the most of your natural gifts. By growing your gifts, you grow the Happiness Habit.

Look around you. How can you be happy …

❖ if you feel frustrated about the opportunities that are closed to you because you do not have the skills
❖ if you feel you are capable of more than you are currently achieving
❖ if you'd like to change aspects of yourself or your life but you don't know how
❖ if you feel life is passing you by and you haven't achieved what you want
❖ if there are no worthwhile challenges in your life that will stretch you
❖ if you haven't explored what you are truly capable of?

Do you feel that you might not have exploited all of your skills, talents and capabilities? Growing as a person is a vital part of feeling good about yourself. Standing still may be comfortable but in the end you will be left feeling slightly cheated.

HAPPY THOUGHT
A happy person knows that in order to grow, you have to feel comfortable being uncomfortable.

How good are you?

Let's start by asking you the question 'What are you good at?'

We have asked many people that question and we are amazed to find that typically people will start by telling us what they are *not* good at. 'Oh, I am hopeless at cooking', 'I never was good at maths', 'I can't draw to save my life', 'I'm not much of a speller' – hold on, stop! That's not what we asked!

What about you? How did you answer the question? Did some of these negatives spring to mind before you could think of all the positives?

The difference between Skills and Capabilities

The first thing to recognise is that there is a difference between Skills and Capabilities. Many people think that because they have never done something then they are not able to do it. We challenge this. Capabilities are the things we are able to do, even if we cannot do them yet. Thus, we are capable of learning new skills if we want to or if we see the need to. For example, just about everyone is *capable* of driving a car, but until they are 18, they cannot legally learn the *skill*. Someone with a bad temper might be *capable* of containing it, but may not see the need to. They would therefore never consider that finding ways to manage their temper would be a good set of skills to learn.

The other thing to be aware of is that sometimes we may have the knowledge but not the skill. We may know exactly what to do, but we don't know how. We need to learn how to translate this knowledge into skilful action if we are to develop our talents to the full.

Creative avoidance

Another way in which we can sabotage our skills development is through creative avoidance. Have you ever had a task to do where you know what to do, you have the skills to do it yet somehow you don't get on with it? You find yourself doing all sorts of other minor tasks that you never had any intention of doing. Although you know you need to do your tax return and time is running out, you tidy the airing cupboard, write thank you letters, walk the dog for the second time that day and sometimes even go so far as doing a different dreaded task – anything is better than the tax return. In cases like this you need to stop and ask yourself, 'What's stopping me?' It may be that you don't believe it's important, you don't think it's your job to do it, or you doubt your own abilities to do it. If this happens it would be a good idea to read the chapter on Beliefs or Identity and see what mental programme is running that is preventing you from making the most of the Skills and Capabilities that you already have.

Learn a new skill

Current research on happiness would suggest that enduring happiness comes from finding opportunities to develop new skills. These challenges might differ depending on what stage of life you are at. Perhaps you are more likely to go bungee jumping or trekking in Borneo when you're under 40 than when you're over 70, however there are no rules. We know an 80-year-old who goes for flying lessons, a couple in their late 70s who go bird watching in the Australian outback in a tent, a woman of 63 who competes in gruelling pentathlons and marathons, a teenager who plays the bagpipes and so on.

What's more important than age is attitude of mind and opportunity. You may never have had the opportunity to learn to ski when you were in your 20s, but later on in life, when you find you have a little more time at your disposal, and enough cash to fund such a hobby, then why not? Don't let social convention hold you back.

Let's face it, most of us want to move on in what we are doing. As soon as something becomes too easy, it becomes routine and dull. Few people would want to keep repeating the same beginner's course in anything. The challenge lies in acquiring new skills and abilities with all of the difficulties that these could encompass. Sometimes the fact that something is hard, requiring real effort, overcoming obstacles and triumphantly reaching a conclusion is what gives a huge injection of happiness.

Achieving success in new areas therefore often requires learning new skills. 'Life Long Learning' is an active campaign of the Department of Learning and Skills. The website www.lifelonglearning.co.uk is dedicated to showing the many different ways that people can acquire new skills that can enhance employment or boost confidence.

Sometimes learning something new can be inspirational and enjoyable in its own right. It doesn't have to have a particular point or Purpose. A book-keeping course can have real fee-earning potential but pottery classes can just be pure fun. There are opportunities everywhere for learning new skills. Night classes, Open University, distance learning, part-time courses, themed holidays, reading something different, listening to radio programmes – these are all ways to increase knowledge and find out what you don't know. As you add to the list of things you can do today that you could not do last year, you will grow in confidence and self-belief. You will gain greater certainty about who you are and what is important to you. You will discard the habits that no longer serve any useful purpose and you will begin to be the person you want to be.

HAPPY THOUGHT
Happiness can be learned.

Happy genes?

Happiness is a skill. Although some people appear to be naturally happier than others, the good news is that happiness is also a skill that can be learned. Some of us may well have inherited a set of happy, cheerful genes. Others, however, simply learned it from their childhood experiences and their upbringing. Can you imagine giving a greater gift to your children and those around you than happiness? We learn by copying what other people do.

By looking on the bright side and being happy, you are showing others the way. The Happiness Habit is learning to behave in an instinctively happy and cheerful way. If you do this consistently, you will feel genuinely happy because what the body does, the mind follows.

Laughing and smiling

Treat smiling and laughing as a skill. Learn to laugh more. Make it a habit. Sometimes life gets so serious we forget how to laugh. We miss out on all the good things laughter brings such as the release of endorphins in the body (providing the same feel-good factor as chocolate but without the calories!), deeper breathing resulting in increased oxygen in the bloodstream giving us greater energy and the release of muscle tension and therefore stress relief. Laughter is a habit. Laughing at misfortune may not always be possible or appropriate – at least at the time – but seeing the funny side of something must surely be better than wallowing in misery.

If you can't laugh, at least try smiling. Find excuses to smile. Do it consciously. The mind and the body are connected. Smiling and laughing help to change our mood and our attitude. Why would you want to be miserable if you could be happy?

HAPPY THOUGHT
Misery is free – and so is happiness!

The happiness paradox

There are two truths at work here which appear to contradict each other but which are actually complementary. Understanding how they work is one of the keys to happiness.

❖ Truth 1

Fake it. Act as if you are happy and you will become happier.

❖ Truth 2

Acknowledge that you are unhappy or have bad feelings. Really feel the feelings.

So if true happiness is dependent on being able to manage that paradox, how is it done?

Truth 1 - Act as if ...

When we say 'Fake it' or 'Pretend...', we don't mean being false or shallow. If your starting point is one of integrity and you are committed to developing your capabilities, this is a perfectly OK and powerful strategy. So if it's important to you to change a habit that makes you miserable, then *acting as if* something is better than it is, is a fabulous starting point.

HAPPY THOUGHT
Learn how to act happy and happiness feelings will follow.

Truth 2 - Feel the feeling

Ignoring negative feelings such as sadness, frustration or anger and pretending they don't exist means that you're not dealing with reality. You're simply stuffing them away inside, where they are likely to fester. There's an increasing amount of research to suggest that negative feelings that are not acknowledged or dealt with appropriately actually reside in parts of the body. Unresolved anger for instance is often connected with heart attacks, and sadness with depression and a weakened immune system.

The ancient Hawaiians spoke about a 'Black Bag' that we all have inside us. Each time we feel a negative or unhappy emotion and we don't want to deal with it, we stuff it into our Black Bag and pull the drawstring tight. The trouble starts when the bag gets too full. The emotions begin to bulge out. The Emotional hijack has just been launched. This can result in embarrassing experiences such as bursting into tears for no apparent reason in front of people we are trying to impress, or losing our cool at just the time we need to be at our most calm.

If there is something that is genuinely upsetting and which is making you feel bad, the important thing is to acknowledge those feelings, feel them and then tell yourself that they will pass. This does not mean wallowing in misery for long periods of time – for this is a habit too. It means being real about your feelings and then using all your mental and emotional skills to get yourself to a better place.

After you have fully acknowledged your feelings, then you'll be in a better position to act as if you are happy. This will be easier and quicker than just ignoring the underlying feelings.

Looking at things differently

If something goes wrong, or something continually nags at you, try looking at it a different way. This works particularly well with small or regular irritations that start off small but somehow grow out of proportion.

Andrea

Andrea was the mother of three children. She had a high profile and demanding job. Every day when she came home from work, tired out, her children would play up and vie for her attention. The same would happen at the weekends. As time went by, Andrea became more and more tired and became resentful of having

---

no time for herself. One day she was visited by a friend who had been trying for a long time to have children and had just been told that this would never happen. After the visit Andrea realised just how fortunate she was to have her three lovely children. Instead of resenting the fact that they wanted her time and attention, she now felt lucky that her children wanted and needed her. This allowed her to be entirely 'present' when talking to and dealing with her children. She would give them her full attention, listen to them more and enjoy their company. Somehow her children became calmer and less demanding.

Looking at things from a different viewpoint is not something than comes easily to everyone. It's a skill that some people seem to have naturally and others have to learn to develop. So, if it's not already in your toolkit, why not practise until it comes naturally to you? It might not solve every problem, but it will help you feel happier about irritating situations that you regularly have to cope with.

HAPPY THOUGHT
It's not the problem, it's the way you look at it that counts.

Using your brain power

How often do you re-live happy moments and experiences in your life? And how often do you re-live unhappy memories? What's the balance between the two? Is it 50/50, or do you think more about distressful events in the past than happy ones?

The brain calls on good memories in order to experience good feelings. It calls on bad memories in order to experience bad feelings. In order therefore to increase the amount of happiness you feel, you need to access more of the positive emotions. These feelings come from responses to things we have experienced in the past. Reliving these experiences will bring the good feelings from the past into the present. This is a skill that will increase the amount of happiness in your life. Using these experiences to develop new perspectives will create new emotional habits. You will be retraining yourself to fire off different habits, different responses and develop a new happiness skill.

Keeping up to date

Keeping up to date is important if you are keen to develop your skills to their full potential. Only 20 years ago who would have believed that a useful skill might be programming your video recorder or your mobile phone? If you don't keep up to date the opportunities for development will pass you by.

It used to be said that an ambitious person keeps a CV in their top drawer. Now everyone should have a CV in their personal file in their computer. It needs to be regularly updated and reviewed so you can measure for yourself your career progression. You know the pace you want to set and you know if you are achieving it.

Taking care of you

We all know the theory of healthy eating and exercise, yet not many of us live it every day of our lives. If we have the sort of bad habits that involve chocolate, alcohol, five course meals or the exercise routine of a couch potato and we want to change, then we need to develop different capabilities or skills.

Learning to look after yourself is part of your development that will lead to greater happiness. If you don't feel well, it is more difficult to feel happy. Looking after yourself may mean gaining new knowledge and skills such as information about additives, colorants and vitamins, alternative therapies, nutrition and dieting, sports and exercise.

Comedy and humour

The power of laughter brings an instant 'feel good' factor. Literature, television, films, radio, clubs, pantomimes, theatre all work on the theme of comedy and laughter. People love to laugh and they can find humour in different situations. What is funny to one person may not be funny to another but think of the most popular films and television shows and most people would agree that they are funny. *Steptoe and Son*, *'Allo 'Allo*, *Dad's Army*, *Fawlty Towers*, *Monty Python*, *Little Britain* and *The Office* have all captured huge audiences because of their ability to make people laugh. Comedians such as John Cleese, Jack Dee and Billy Connolly have the extraordinary skill to make audiences helpless with laughter. Catch phrases from shows enter the English language and suddenly all you have to say is 'He's from Barcelona' and we are all laughing – Manuel from Fawlty Towers has made his mark.

Jokes do the rounds by word of mouth, the internet, television and mobile phone. The objective is to make people laugh, but why is this? To make people temporarily forget their problems and to release the pressure from potentially difficult situations. We laugh at someone slipping on a banana skin just as we laugh at a sophisticated and witty talk. Whatever the source and whatever the delivery, humour is the key to lifting the spirits and equates to a moment in time when you can claim to be happy.

Laughing gas

The Victorians knew how to short-cut their way to laughter and give themselves a dose of instant happiness. A popular pastime in Victorian Britain was the Grand Exhibitions, travelling medicine shows and carnivals where Nitrous Oxide was administered to eager members of the audience. The result was that people would laugh and act silly until the effects of the drug came to an abrupt end and they would stand about in confusion. In a flier for a Victorian laughter evening, the event was advertised as, 'Those who inhale the Gas once are always anxious to inhale it the second time'. So much for grandly sweeping aside the addictive properties of a drug that while it induces helpless laughter, can also kill. It brings new meaning to the phrase, 'I nearly died laughing!' It is well known that laughter has many benefits including strengthening your immune system, increasing your intellectual performance and helping your memory. If in doubt, laugh – but do it naturally!

Flexibility

HAPPY THOUGHT
The more skills you have to play with, the more likely you are to get the results you want.

Skills give us flexibility. If we're not getting the happiness we want and we don't know how to change what we're doing, then things are not likely to change for the better. This applies in all aspects of our lives – whether it's how to make more money, how to create happier and better relationships, how to keep healthy, how to enjoy the work we do and so on.

If the only tool in your toolbox is a hammer, then pretty soon everything begins to look like a nail.

Relationships

You need a huge raft of skills to make relationships work well. An added complication is looking at what we mean by relationships. We mean partner, wife, husband, boyfriend, girlfriend, relatives, friends, colleagues, acquaintances, plus all of those ad-hoc, one-off conversations or encounters that make up daily life. Harmony in relationships right across the board is a vital ingredient of happiness. A short-tempered encounter can unsettle you for the day, so learning how to manage relationships with others in order to get the best out of them is a life skill no one can do without. What many people do not know is that there are techniques you can learn. You will find some of them in the Brilliant Ideas.

Money

We know that money alone does not create happiness but a lack of it can certainly lead to unhappiness. We also know that money doesn't just drop into our laps. The decisions we make about our education, our relationships, our careers and our families have direct financial consequences. How we choose to lead our lives and deal with money can mean a life where lack of funds will constantly be an anxiety and a problem or, alternatively, where skillfully managed money can reduce the sort of problems that result in unhappiness. Despite knowing all this instinctively, we still look to money as the gateway to happiness.

HAPPY THOUGHT
'Money can't buy you love.'

The lottery and the road to happiness

Is money the root of all evil or is it the road to happiness? Every week, millions of people in Britain buy lottery tickets believing that if they get that winning ticket, their problems will be over.

Money will give them the key to the happiness door, removing anxiety about bills or lack of cash and it will enable them to live their dreams, exploit their potential and pave the way to Shangri-La.

The National Lottery commissioned MORI to carry out a survey on major lottery winners to find out what impact the money had on their lifestyle. In particular they asked if the money made them happy. The results are given here.

- ❖ Since winning the jackpot, 35% of lottery winners were as happy and 65% were happier than before.
- ❖ The reasons for being happier included financial security (64%), being able to do and buy what they liked (43%) and enjoying an easier life (23%).
- ❖ Lack of pressure, stress and worries (28%), being able to give up work (14%) and looking after family and friends (13%) were deemed the best things to happen after a win.
- ❖ 92% of winners who were married when they won are still married to the same person.

On the surface, the answer would therefore seem to be clear – money makes you happier. Intriguingly, all of us, aspiring lottery winners included, want to pay off mortgages, buy a bigger house with a new car on the drive, go on holiday a lot, give money away to families and friends and buy a house in the sun. Thirty-four per cent of lottery big winners have gone on a cruise, so we all seem to believe that freedom from anxiety about money, combined with the material possessions that bring comfort and security, will rocket us to the certainty of happiness.

We now know why people buy a lottery ticket week after week. They are pursuing a dream that will allow them to short-circuit the conventional path to happiness. A cheque with a huge amount of noughts on the end will mean that they no longer need to think about work, a career, making ends meet, juggling finances and dealing with the daily task of survival. For most of us who won't win the lottery then, the challenge would seem to be how to convert everyday working life into something that is enjoyable and that also generates enough money to remove the financial worries from life.

Brilliant Ideas to develop the Happiness Habit in your Skills and Capabilities - it will only take you 21 days!

/ The useful CV

For many people, the way to increasing their quality of life and to gain freedom from financial concerns is through their work. Moving jobs is one way to progress your career and increase your earning power.

The first Step when you are off to find a new job is to have your CV right. Here are a few practical tips to help you put it together.

First of all, when you write your CV, make sure you list what you are achieving in your current role, rather than what you are responsible for. Include a section on leisure pursuits and see how they stack up. When did you last try something new? What have you got on that list that gives you a sense of deep satisfaction? Try writing the leisure pursuits as you would like them to be, rather than how they are. What do they look like now? What is preventing you from doing them? Often the hustle and bustle of daily life stops us from taking the time we should have for ourselves.

A good CV is one that is clear, objective and gives a picture of who you are to a reader. It gives a chronological sequence of events and learning. When you look at yours, is it showing you as you want to be? Are you demonstrating that you have a curious mind and you are constantly learning or are you doing the same this year as you did last?

Use the exercise of updating your CV as an opportunity to evaluate where you are in life. The CV is the practical tool you need to apply for a new job. It is also your own personal barometer on what is happening in your life.

2 Pick a skill

Think of something you have always wanted to do but never thought you were good enough to do it. It could be a sport or activity such as golf, yoga, swimming, football, running, rock climbing, sailing, windsurfing, or it could be learning a language, writing short stories, painting, salsa dancing, surfing the web, practical DIY, driving a car or riding a bike. It can be anything. Choose what skill you would love to have if only you had the time, the knowledge, the ability, the money or anything else that could be holding you back. Then decide to do it. Find a way to manage the time and the money and give yourself the thrill of doing what you love.

The result will be a boost of self-confidence, a lifting of the spirits, a surge in energy – and happiness!

3 How to do instant happiness

- ❖ Smile – even when you don't feel like it. It's hard to feel miserable if your muscles are in the smiling position. Try it and see!
- ❖ Stand up straight and keep your chin up – or look up. Again, it's hard to feel miserable in this position. Your mind and your body are connected. If your body is in the happiness posture, your mind will follow.
- ❖ Fake it! Act as if you are happy or that things are a lot happier than they are. Your mind cannot tell the difference between what's real and what you imagine.

- ❖ Make a point of smiling at people – even ones you don't know. This of course could get you into trouble, so choose wisely! Smiling and saying hello to a group of walkers that you pass on a hillside might be a little safer than saying hello to the person next to you on the Tube or the bus where your friendliness could be misinterpreted. Smile at the antics of children playing. Smile at the person who cuts you up on the motorway. Smile at the cashier at the petrol station when you pay them. Smile at your partner when you get home after a trying and frustrating day at work.

4 Look after your physical health

Your physical health gives you energy. Tiredness makes it hard to cope and keep cheerful when times are tough. Looking after yourself gives you more of the resources you need to keep your mental energy high

Here are some suggestions on how to look after yourself that will have a positive effect on your state of mind and therefore your happiness.

- ❖ Decide that prevention is better than cure and don't wait till you're ill before making health a priority.
- ❖ Learn to listen to your body so you know when you need more sleep, more exercise, or when you need to go to the doctors.
- ❖ Learn to cook healthy meals.
- ❖ Find out about food additives and colourings and read food labels, so you are aware of any added salt or sugar.
- ❖ Monitor the effect of certain foods and drinks on your energy levels and moods.
- ❖ Go to classes to learn how to be fit in ways that you enjoy – whether it's aerobics, swimming, body building, team games, golf, racket games, walking or judo.

- ❖ Take regular breaks during a long working day.
- ❖ In your job, be sure to use up your holiday entitlement.

5 Look after your mental health

- ❖ Explore the wide variety of relaxation techniques and classes around. Learn how to recharge your mental batteries.
- ❖ Practise stilling the busyness in your mind through meditation or simply by sitting and doing nothing for a few minutes.
- ❖ Notice beautiful things such as the detail of a flower, the movements of a bird, the expressions on a baby's face, the colours of a sunset, the detail of a painting or a sculpture.
- ❖ Build in time to visit places of peace or spiritual inspiration – e.g. holy places such as abbey ruins and cathedrals or natural beauty spots such as waterfalls or lakes.
- ❖ Read books and watch films that are uplifting, inspirational and are food for the soul.

6 Laugh it off

Decide that you will work to find the funny side in situations. Start with the small things and get into the habit of seeing the amusing side and laughing things off. Ask yourself, 'What's the funny side of this?' or 'When will this be funny?' Soon you will be able to laugh things off more than you could before.

7 Happy hour

Pubs and bars have created 'Happy Hour', a fixed time, usually in the early evening, when drinks are served half price or two for the price of one. People make a point of visiting the bar at that particular time in order to enjoy Happy Hour. Create your own Happy Hour when you will be focusing your energy on being happy. Instead of allowing yourself twice the amount of alcohol, allow yourself double the quantity of time doing what really makes you happy.

8 Misery hour

If something is upsetting you badly, why not set aside a time when you can allow yourself to feel really miserable. For example spend an hour being upset and feeling the negative feelings. The great thing about this is that it's hard to sustain peak emotions for lengthy periods of time – whether they are positive or negative. At the end of the hour (or whatever timescale is right for you) you are likely to feel more ready to leave those feelings behind and begin to feel better.

9 Train your brain

When things are going badly and looking bleak, take time out to think of a number of occasions that were happy experiences. They don't have to be earth shattering but they do need to be meaningful. For example, remember the time your baby was born, when you saw a stunning view, when you recognised true love. Soon your brain will be trained to look for and recapture positive feelings instead of negative ones.

10 Sunny side up

When faced with regular or irritating situations, ask yourself, 'How can I look at this situation differently? What's good about it? What would make me feel better about it?' Make a list and then approach the situation from a more positive starting point. This is one of the key ways to experience real happiness every day of your life.

11 Keep up to date

Keep testing and sharpening your skills by keeping up to date with what's going on around you. Not only will that increase your quality of life by keeping you sharp and active, but it will also make you feel good that you are taking on new challenges successfully. Ways you can keep up to date might include keeping up to date with technology. For example, learning new computer programmes and skills, installing and using Wi Fi technology, buying yourself an iPod to replace your Walkman, sending e-mails as well as writing notes, buying a digital camera and downloading your pictures onto a computer.

Keep up to date with the latest developments in the news, in the arts world and in your line of business – you could read relevant business or trade magazines rather than throwing them in the bin or filing them unopened. Read a variety of different newspapers and news magazines; listen to different news channels on the TV and radio. Don't stick to the same old ones. Read different authors and different types of books and try going to the opera as well as the theatre or the cinema. Try doing different types of crossword puzzles and teach yourself to become a Sudoku master.

Not only will these give you more knowledge and skills that will give you satisfaction, they will help you develop and grow the skill of creating new and better habits.

12 Develop your relationships

❖ Move your relationships to a different level by doing things differently. You could try saying what you want and need from the other person in order to gain greater happiness from the relationship. You can also ask the other person what they need from *you* in order for the relationship to work better.

- ❖ Develop assertiveness skills. Learn to ask for what you want and need and do not rely on telepathy! Say clearly what is unacceptable in the relationship and tell the person – politely but firmly.
- ❖ Develop your listening skills. A sympathetic ear is sometimes all that's needed when a close friend or partner has a problem. Jumping in to solve a problem sometimes does more harm than good.
- ❖ Ask people for feedback about how you come across. Brace yourself before you do and make sure you are ready to hear criticisms as well as praise. It's important here to choose wisely so that the feedback you get is honest and is also considerate of your feelings.

13 Increase your well-being

Make a list of the habits you have that are affecting your health and well-being. Pick the top two or three. Now decide what specifically you need to learn about in order to get rid of these unhealthy habits. Finally, start the ball rolling to gain this new knowledge or skill by taking your first action today.

14 Time to laugh

If you are finding it hard to lift a black mood, get hold of a funny book or a film or a re-run of a classic comedy programme and immerse yourself in it. You won't be able to sustain a dark mood for long in the face of a barrage of humour!

15 Emotional resilience

Learn the skill of bouncing back. When the odds are stacked against you, remember the critical question, 'Who can I get to help me?'

WORK BOOK

Workbook Step 3 – Skills and Capabilities

Guide to using the Workbook

When you are going through this Workbook, you will find some of the questions easier than others. Sometimes the answers will spring instantly to mind. Other times you may need to take time out to reflect and consider what this could mean for you.

You may find it useful to go through a checklist of the areas that could affect your happiness. When answering these questions, some of the things to consider would be how your Skills and Capabilities (or lack of them) affect:

❖ your relationships
❖ your money
❖ your work
❖ your health.

This is about your talents and your personal development and how they affect your happiness.

A What are the **three** things that you are best at that make you feel proud and happy?

1 ....

....

....

2 ....

....

....

3 ....

....

....

B What are the **three** skills that you wish you could have,
   that you know in your heart-of-hearts would make
   you happy?

1 ....

....

....

2 ....

....

....

3 ....

....

....

C What talents do you have that you are not using that,
   if you did, would make you feel a lot happier?

1 ....

....

....

2 ....

....

....

3 ....

....

....

D What are those hidden talents which, if you used
   them, could make you more fulfilled and happy?

1 ....

....

....

2 ....

....

....

3 ....

....

....

5 What **one** thing could you ask somebody to do to help you grow your talents?

....

....

....

Think hard about what you have written above. Decide now what actions you will take to develop those Skills and Capabilities which are most likely to add to your happiness. Make sure you write them down.

Actions:

....

....

....

The Happiness Challenge for Step 3 on the Stairway of Happiness - Skills and Capabilities

THE HAPPINESS MANTRA

Your happiness state will only change if you do things differently and if you increase the number of Happiness Habits you develop. Remember it takes only 21 days to create permanent change.

In order to increase your happiness, take the Happiness Challenge.

Take one of the actions that you have identified in this Workbook. Every day for 21 days, stop just thinking about making this change. Go out and do it!

New habit to be developed

....

....

....

Keep a check on your progress. Put a tick in the box every day for 21 days when you have practised that habit.

Progress Chart						
Day 1	Day 2	Day 3	Day 4	Day 5	Day 6	Day 7
Day 8	Day 9	Day 10	Day 11	Day 12	Day 13	Day 14
Day 15	Day 16	Day 17	Day 18	Day 19	Day 20	Day 21

Start date ....

6

Values and Beliefs

The Fourth Step on the Stairway of Happiness

You're now at the critical point where you will be looking at what is really important to you in your life. Now you can ask yourself if you know what really matters to you in life and if you're living your life that way.

Remember! To make lasting changes to your happiness by ensuring you're living your life in line with what is truly important to you, you may need to work at one Step above on the Stairway of Happiness. This means that in order to recognise the real values in your life and to gain passion and energy from them, you need to know who you are and be able to accept yourself.

Step 6 – Purpose
Purpose is what brings meaning into your life. It's why you are here.

Step 5 – Identity
Identity is about acknowledging your roots and accepting yourself for who you are.

Step 4 – Values and Beliefs
Values and Beliefs are the programming, power, motivation and energy behind your actions.

Step 3 – Skills and Capabilities
Skills and Capabilities are all the talents you have or could have, given the opportunity.

Step 2 – Behaviour
Behaviour includes what you do, how you do it, who you do it with and how others behave with you. It's also about what you think, what you say and how you say it.

Step 1 – Surroundings
Your Surroundings are everything you see, hear and feel when you look around you. It's your environment and the results you are getting.

Values and Beliefs

Values and Beliefs are the programming, the power and the motivation for what we do in our daily lives. They provide the energy and the drive and the passion behind our actions. Our values are the things that are important to us. This can include things such as harmony, security, health, freedom, honesty, trust, family, generosity, openness, cleanliness, orderliness, organisation, variety, impulsiveness, options – the list is endless – and it's also personal. Beliefs are our truths. They can be our guidelines, our rules or our justification for the things we do. Living life in line with our values is essential for happiness.

Look around you. How can you feel happy about the path you are following …

❖ if you cannot find the energy and the motivation to get on with life
❖ if you're unhappy with how you're living, perhaps allowing yourself to do things that you feel uneasy with
❖ if you're going along with a way of life that does not fit with what is important to you
❖ if you're doing something that feels somehow wrong for you
❖ if someone else's values are overshadowing yours so that your way of life has been chosen by someone else?

Be true to yourself

What is important to you in your life? What is really important to you in your life? Have you ever taken the time to think about these things, to work out exactly what they are and then make sure that you're giving them enough time? The day-to-day pressures of everyday life often absorb the precious time we could give to what really matters. Positive beliefs about ourselves and others are the best starting point for happiness.

As a happy person you will be true to yourself. You will be clear about what you believe in and what you value in life and you won't allow yourself to be swayed by other people or external events.

If your beliefs and values are not working for you, then you need to make changes at the level above – Identity. As you read through his chapter, think about the impact that positive and negative beliefs have on your whole life – the skills and abilities you believe you can acquire, the behaviours you adopt.

Values and beliefs may not be something we think about consciously in our day-to-day lives. However, their impact is fundamental to the amount of happiness in our lives. Think about your values and beliefs as being like the engine in a car or the software programme driving your computer. When you're driving your car or working on your computer, you know that the power is coming from a source you can't see. You don't consciously think about it but you know it's critical to the action. The size and type of the engine in a car will dictate its performance; how fast it can go, how many miles it does to the gallon, how fast it can take a corner, how safe it is in an accident and even how the driver will be perceived by other road users and friends. It's the same with a computer – you're restricted to what you can do by what the software programme includes. You won't be able to transfer music on to your iPod if you don't have the right programme on your computer, and the iPod won't work at its best.

Programming and power

Values and Beliefs are therefore the programming, the power and the motivation for what we do in our daily lives. They provide the motivation to do or not do things in our lives. If you believe that exercise is a vital part of leading a healthy life, you will go jogging, play football, go for walks, go to yoga classes, go swimming or go to a gym. You will feel happy because it's important to you to integrate exercise into your routine. If you miss it out because you're too busy or on holiday, then you will be unhappy and may feel guilty that you're not doing something that is really important to you.

Some people will be equally highly motivated not to do anything that smacks of excess expenditure of energy and will never bother – exercise is low down their value set and it does not show up on the radar screen of their happiness.

Two of the most common values are those of achievement and challenge. If you ask someone what motivates them or why they want to change jobs, the most frequent reply is, 'I'm looking for a new challenge' or 'I feel I've achieved all I can in my current job, so I am looking for a position that will allow me to contribute more'. Outside the work scene, challenge is also a great motivator. Just think how many people enter for the London Marathon or who are motivated to do crazy things to achieve an entry in the *Guinness Book of Records*. They are programmed by their values.

The stronger the value, the stronger the motivation.

The fruit tree

Values are the branches that beliefs hang on. It's rather like the fruit hanging on the branches of a tree. Each branch is a value and each piece of fruit on that branch is a belief. So for example, if you value safety, you are likely to believe that it's important to:

- ❖ buy a car with excellent safety features
- ❖ ensure your home is secure and well protected
- ❖ follow health and safety rules and regulations
- ❖ drive carefully.

If you value personal development, you are likely to believe that it's important to buy books to expand your development in areas that you're interested in and to look for opportunities to increase your knowledge or education.

Believe it or not

Beliefs are what we hold to be true. They drive our behaviour. So, for example if you have a strong religious belief, you are likely to go to a place of worship regularly and to believe in the power of prayer. If you don't believe in a God or have a faith of any sort, then it won't form part of your life.

Because you believe that the concepts and ideas in this book are likely to work, then you will be more likely to try them out. They are more likely to work and you are likely to become happier. If you believe, for whatever reason that happiness is not your lot, you are less likely to find it than if you do.

Isn't it great to know that we can all choose our beliefs and we can choose what we don't believe in? We can weed out those that are out of date or which are not working for us. Now of course, for deeply rooted negative beliefs, this may take a little longer, but just to know that it's possible and to keep an open mind about what might work is a great starting point. Bear in mind that it only takes 21 days to change a habit. Who knows where it might lead!

Feng Shui or not

If you value cleanliness and tidiness, you're likely to make sure your house is clean and that you're living in a tidy home or an orderly office. If you're sitting in a mess with papers strewn everywhere and things lying around, it could be a source of stress for you and stand in the way of a feeling of happiness. The disorder will just get in the way of what you want to do. Some of you, however, don't value neatness and order. You just thrive on chaos, loving having everything around, unconcerned about piles of things on chairs and ironing baskets full to overflowing. Feng Shui is a mystery to you and you won't see its point. Disorder is a source of inspiration and energy for you.

Looking good

For some people looking good is very important and it has a high value for them. Taking care of themselves is high up their priority list and they are miserable if they feel they are letting themselves go. If you're like this then it may mean that you're keen on exercise or spend a lot of money on clothes, make-up, haircuts, beauty sessions. Maintaining good looks and a youthful appearance may contribute to your overall feeling of happiness.

Financial beliefs

Money is often seen as the gateway to happiness – and it is true that it can certainly make life more comfortable. It provides us with many of those external pleasures that we associate with happiness. In the pursuit of this kind of happiness many people actually end up in misery.

Overspending and racking up credit card bills is rife. Credit card debt increased by 16% in the UK last year and bankruptcy is common. Recent research tells us that many people who are struggling with debt are aged under 30 and owe up to £60 000 each. Students take on loans and overdrafts in order to go to university and get a degree and they become accustomed to living in debt.

Money was no object!

Tony is 24 and believes that happiness comes from the pursuit of personal enjoyment and that the world owes him a living. He knows what he wants and he wants it now. His parents are well off and he is accustomed to the material benefits of life. Because of this, he goes out monthly and spends whatever he wants on entertainment, clothes and travel. Every month he spends more than double his salary, so he regularly increases his overdraft limit and the number of credit cards he holds.

This worked very well for a period, but there came a time when his creditors demanded payment. He reached a point when he dreaded the arrival of the post in the morning and became stressed and depressed. Tony cheered himself up by spending even more until eventually all lines of credit ran out. Finally, he went to his wealthy parents to ask for help. They were stunned by his level of debt and reluctantly, agreed to repay the debt on condition that Tony agreed to learn his lesson and mend his ways. Tony agreed.

> One year later, Tony was in exactly the same position as before. Why had his behaviour not changed? Simply because his belief that somehow or other he 'should have' all the good things in life had not changed. He did not properly value the gift his parents had given him. He believed that somehow good things in life came on a plate and were his by right.

The pursuit of pleasure that is not based on true beliefs and has no regard to the consequences may seem like a happy way to live. Long term, however, this is simply a recipe for serial disappointment and unhappiness. The pursuit of pleasure is not happiness. Don't confuse short-term pleasures from external sources with real happiness.

Mr Micawber, in the novel *David Copperfield* by Charles Dickens, gave some shrewd advice:

> Annual income twenty pounds, annual expenditure nineteen nineteen six, result happiness. Annual income twenty pounds, annual expenditure twenty pounds nought and six, result misery.

Beliefs about relationships

What do you believe about yourself?

Some people wonder why they continually attract the wrong kind of person and end up in relationships which are unsuitable, miserable, dissatisfying, born for failure or even abusive. Often this can be tracked back to the sort of beliefs people have. These beliefs may be about the sort of partner they deserve, the sort of person they are, or they may simply believe that they are unlucky in love based on one or more previous experiences. If you believe that you are not good at relationships, this will affect the sort of person you are attracted to and the sort of person who finds you attractive. You're also likely to screen out the things that go well and to focus on the things that go wrong in your relationships. It's almost as if you're willing it to fail. The result you will get is another unsatisfactory relationship that will simply reinforce what you believe about your lack of ability to maintain relationships. The self-fulfilling prophecy is born.

On the other hand, believe that you deserve nothing but the best and that you know how to find it, and this will come your way.

Beliefs and health

Believe you are ill and you certainly will be so. We all know this to be true in small ways. People who enjoy the best of health when they are at work suddenly develop colds or coughs when they are on holiday. Teachers who believe that it's not acceptable to be ill during the school term postpone their illness till the holiday period. It's as though it's being stored up and just waiting for you to relax. You believe you can't be ill when you're working but you haven't decided yet that you can't be ill when you're on holiday.

The pharmacy of the brain

Each of us has our own personal pharmacy in the brain. What we believe and what we think trigger off certain physical reactions. This in turn allows the brain to drip feed us with natural chemicals. Positive thoughts and beliefs help the brain secrete wonderful endorphins into our body. These produce a feel-good factor, help our immune system, and make us less vulnerable to illness. On the other hand, if our beliefs are unhelpful or negative, different chemicals are sent from the brain to the body. Result? Our immune system is less robust and we are more open to germs, viruses and other complaints. Which would you rather have?

What we believe about other people

What we believe about other people is also critical to our happiness. Albert Einstein, when asked the question, 'What is the most important question a human being can answer?' said, 'Is the world a friendly place or not?'

If we believe that the world is unfriendly, then the things that people say and do to us are likely to be interpreted negatively. This is the pathway to a sad existence. On the contrary, if we believe that most people in the world are friendly, decent people, then we are likely to see the best in people and events. This is not as naive and trusting as it sounds. The fact that occasionally you are let down allows you to put more faith and trust in others. We are likely to find more friendship, more satisfaction and more happiness if this is our mental starting point.

Happiness does not depend on external events, but hinges on how we look at them.

Happiness - the Peak State

Just before a race, athletes concentrate on getting themselves into Peak State, the positive trance-like feeling where they focus only on the goal in hand and which gives them the best chance of winning. They filter out everything except the race, the state they are in and the desire to win. Footballers before the game concentrate on getting themselves into that Peak State where they will play the best they ever have and their team will win the game.

Now in the race of life we can do the same thing. Being in a Peak State is a state of happiness. When we are in this Peak State it's impossible to feel negative or unhappy. This is because we are in the moment. The past does not exist and the future has not yet arrived. Just think of times in your life when you were having a wonderful time. You probably didn't think to yourself 'I'm happy!' You were just enjoying being in the present – or, as it's sometimes called, being 'in the now'. The feeling of being in the moment can range from feelings of ecstasy and excitement, to simply warm feelings of well-being

If you want, you can choose what you focus on in just the same way as athletes do before a race and gain the best results.

Our energy goes where our focus goes.

When you are remembering the past or thinking about the future, you are not in Peak State. You can't be in Peak State all the time but equally however you can decide to spend less time buried in the past or to be less preoccupied with the future. It's a question of balance. The impact on your happiness hinges on whether your focus is positive or negative. Have a look at the table below.

	The Past	The Present	The Future
If your focus is positive …	… you look to the past as a means of reference and learning. You know that the past does not equal the future. You focus on the good memories.	… you are in 'the moment/in Peak State'. You are focused on *the now,* but at the same time you are alert to what's going on around you. You are receptive and flexible. Your antennae are out!	… you are clear what your goals are. They motivate you and bring meaning to the present. You look forward to the future with keen anticipation.
If your focus is negative …	… you spend too much time living in the past, focusing on and re-living bad times and events.	… you are bogged down with the difficulties of the present. You cannot see the wood for the trees. You are in overwhelm. In extreme form this can result in mental illness and even suicide.	… either you are so caught up in the future that you are out of touch with the real world – OR – perhaps you are frozen with anxiety so that you simply cannot move forward or fulfil your potential.

As the poet Robert Burns said:

> But, och! I backward cast my e'e
> On prospects drear
> An' forward, tho' I canna see,
> I guess an' fear!

Our beliefs act as filters. We screen out information that does not match with our beliefs.

Good citizens

Have you ever wondered why so many people get involved in voluntary or charity work? Why do they do it? What is motivating them to do something so selfless?

This is different for everybody. Take Lucy for instance. She is mother of two small children and does not do paid work. However she gives hours of her time to organising and running high-profile events for a children's charity throughout the year. She raises funds tirelessly and drives her fund-raising commitment to ever greater heights. Nothing puts her off. The endless organisation and administration never seem to bother her. The knock-backs and rebuffs do not deter her. Why does she do it? Because recognition and appreciation are core values for her. She gets her happiness buzz from the praise of others, her picture in the local paper and the knowledge that she is making a great contribution to a worthwhile cause. One day she may be awarded an MBE or OBE that will make her even happier.

Similarly, James is a magistrate – a position of high status which is voluntary and unpaid. Although he is in full-time employment and holds a senior management role, he wants to make a positive contribution to the community. He values activities that make him feel like a worthwhile person. This is what motivates him to give up much of his limited free time to an unpaid activity. He needs the approbation and admiration of others to help build his self-esteem.

Greg is different. He is motivated by achievement. Achievement makes him happy. He has just set up his own business and his long-term goal is to be so successful that he can buy himself a Porsche. Joe on the other hand, a friend of his from a well-to-do family, was given a Porsche for his birthday by his doting parents. Was Greg jealous? No! What he said was, 'I wouldn't want anyone to give me a Porsche because it wouldn't mean as much. When I get my Porsche I know I will have earned every bit of it.' Greg's drive and energy comes from a desire to achieve. The material goal in itself is almost irrelevant, as paradoxically if it were given to him, it would either lead to demotivation and feelings of vague unhappiness or he would immediately substitute that goal with another.

Values and decisions

An insight into our own values will be a critical aid in helping us to make decisions, especially at key crossroads in our lives. Good decisions lead to happiness.

As Leo Tolstoy, the novelist and philosopher said, 'Decisions are easy when values are clear.'

Weighing up the pros and cons

Jenny worked as a clerical assistant in a small, well-established company. She loved the teamwork and feeling that she was contributing to the success of the company. Her job was as secure as any job is and she valued the fact it was near to home, so that she could make the most of her leisure time. The job was therefore matching three key values – being part of a team, security and having leisure time.

A job came up paying much more money in a large new company at a salary considerably more than the one Jenny was on. She applied for it, knowing that it would enable her to get a mortgage, and would place her further up the career ladder. However, the offices were further away so it would mean a longer commute in the morning and the job itself involved a lot of travelling. This new job was therefore offering her the opportunity to match up to two different values that she held – being able to afford to buy her own home and advancing her career.

To her surprise and delight, she was offered the post. She was even more surprised to find herself considering whether she wanted to accept it or not. She found herself weighing up the advantages and disadvantages of both jobs and what they would mean for her life. To make her decision she wrote a list of the values that each job would satisfy and worked out which had the most weighting for her. In the end she accepted the post, as she realised that getting on in her career and being successful were the two most important values at that time in her life.

Brilliant Ideas to develop the Happiness Habit in your Values and Beliefs – it will only take you 21 days!

1 How to check out your own values

People with a strong set of values may not be able to articulate them easily. They may never have sat down to analyse what their values are. They simply feel strongly about how they would like to do something. Being clear about your values and having a set of values that work for you is a definite road to happiness. So how do you find out what our values are? Easy! Just ask yourself this key question.

'What are some of the things that are important to me in my life?' Write them down, then reorganise them in terms of importance.

1 ....
....

2 ....
....

3 ....
....

4 ....
....

5 ....
....

6 ....
....

7 ....
....

8 ....
....

9 ....
....

Now choose one of the values that you have written down and follow through with the questions in the way illustrated below.

Let's say that having asked yourself the key question, 'What are some of the things that are important to me in my life?' and one of your first answers to the question is, 'Money'.

Now imagine we were talking. The conversation might go something like this.

> **Heather and Anne:** So tell us in your own words – why is making money important to you?
>
> **You:** Because the way I think of it, money equals success. I'll feel I've actually achieved something in life if I become wealthy.

Heather and Anne: This may sound like an odd question, but what does success do for you? Why is that important to you?

You: It makes me feel good about myself.

Now in this case, money (actually success) is the value we are exploring. By digging a little deeper than the first reply, we have discovered that your value of Success brings you good feelings, i.e. it makes you happy.

Equally, the conversation could have gone as follows.

Heather and Anne: So tell us in your own words – why is money important to you?

You: Because the way I think of it, money equals success. I'll feel I've actually achieved something in life if I become wealthy.

Heather and Anne: This may sound like an odd question, but what does success do for you? Why is that important to you?

You: I don't want to be a failure.

In this instance, your apparent value of money (actually success) is motivating because its purpose is to take you away from the pain, the bad feelings of unhappiness.

Now if you try this out on any value you care to test it out on – our bet is that you will reach a similar result if you dig deep enough. Our values motivate us because they result in good feelings, i.e. happiness, OR they reduce bad feelings and so allow us to feel good.

To achieve a point therefore where we feel happy when we feel good about ourselves and inside ourselves, we need to access what our values are.

Happiness is the value we are all striving to reach. Unhappiness is the state we are motivated to get away from.

2 Just a little bit extra

Money is what will either enable you to live in line with your values and beliefs or will hold you back. It will be a source of stress and worry, draining your energy and stopping you from concentrating, or it will make you happy.

If you need more money to live the life you want to lead, you could use these ideas to add to your cash pot.

- ❖ Clear out your house of unwanted items and sell them on eBay® or at a car boot sale. Now is the time to find all those unused bikes, toys, books, china, hi-fi systems, radios, microwaves, etc. and convert them into cash.
- ❖ See if you can work extra hours and earn some over-time.
- ❖ Decide to create meals out of what you have in the cupboards and buy ingredients only when you need them.
- ❖ If you have a talent, make it work for you financially. This could mean selling your paintings, using your DIY skills in other people's homes, selling your plants or marketing your pottery.
- ❖ Enter competitions in magazines and see if you win. Someone has to win, so why shouldn't it be you?

3 The power of money to hijack happiness

If you are caught in a trap of finances spiralling out of control, robbing one credit card to pay the minimum amount on another with fears about money constantly at the forefront of your mind, what can you do about it? Well first you need to check out what you believe about money, what you believe about yourself and so on. Then perhaps you need to change your thinking. Alter your attitude to money and spending and then you will be able to alter the behaviour that affects your spending pattern.

You can then start by taking the following sort of actions.

- ❖ Stop taking out more credit cards.
- ❖ If you can, cut up the ones that you have so that you can no longer use them.
- ❖ Make life simpler by consolidating your bank accounts and credit cards.
- ❖ Practise self-restraint. Ask yourself before buying something, 'Do I really need this? Do I have to spend this money? What other choices do I have? What could I do instead?'
- ❖ Make it a priority to pay off your debts and keep within a known budget.
- ❖ Create a daily spending log so that you can see exactly where every penny is going.
- ❖ Set up a system of automatic payments and budget round those. This will help you work towards a more solid and satisfactory financial position.
- ❖ Have you got the best mortgage deal? Take advice and see if you can save.
- ❖ Are you making the best use of your assets? Could you rent out a bedroom?
- ❖ Contact someone with financial planning expertise to help you design a way of managing your finances that works for you.
- ❖ If you're seriously worried, get in touch with the Citizen's Advice Bureau to help you devise a new strategy.

4 How to get into Peak State

All of these world class sportspeople must know what they are doing. They have spent their careers to date making sure they are in Peak State when they need to be so that they can win, know success and be happy.

When you're in a Peak State, it's as if your senses have been magnified. You can see and hear things clearly, you can concentrate on one thing but you are also very aware of everything that's going on around you. To get into that state on purpose, sit or stand and look slightly upwards – just above eye level and gently defocus your eyes. Notice that you can focus on a particular object or spot and that at the same time you are very aware of everything that's going on around you. If at that point you have a goal in mind, your mind will be sharp and your body energised and motivated to take whatever action you need to progress towards your goal.

Now think of something you want to do. Get into Peak State and see what a difference it makes. Do this every day for 21 days and incorporate Peak State into how you think and how you behave.

5 How to get into the moment

If you want to be happy, it's important to try out new techniques. This exercise is a way of practicing being where you are now rather than focusing on the past or the future.

Sit comfortably, move one arm out to your side. Move your hand from the side towards your heart taking two minutes to complete the 'journey'. Notice thoughts, images and feelings while doing the exercise.

6 The decision maker

When faced with a life decision and you're not sure which road to take, one way to help you decide is to check out which decision is most in line with your values. If one decision satisfies one value and another decision satisfies a different one, then the solution here is to be clear about which value matters more. As you have already worked out the priority of your values by doing our first

Brilliant Idea, you will know which one is the most important to you and your decision will be easier.

7 Be willing to change

If you're wondering if your current values and beliefs are still working for you, be ready to change. Something that may have stood you in good stead when you were single may not be right for you for you when you're married with children. Flexibility is a great tool to help you be happy. If you stick rigidly to a way and a pattern of doing things, it may stand in your way.

8 Look around you

Remember to look at people you know and admire and work out what seems to be driving them. Think whether or not you could try it for yourself. If a partner goes to church and you do not, maybe you could go along too and see if it worked for you. If you have never gone running, try it out and see if you feel better if you incorporate physical fitness into your values. Think of someone you admire. Work out what they do, what they say, what they think or how they go about things and decide to be the same yourself.

9 The jelly mould

Each of us has a set of Values and Beliefs that are unique to us. It's rather as if we have our own jelly mould and we believe that it's the only one that has merit. When other people do things that don't fit with our jelly mould we get upset, disappointed, frustrated and angry. We expect other people to say and do the things that we would say or do ourselves. These negative feelings detract from our potential for happiness. Unfortunately for us, other people also have their own unique jelly moulds where their values and beliefs may be very different to ours. Imagine a jelly on a plate that is large round and smooth. You don't like the size or shape so you place your own fancy square jelly mould over their jelly to try to make it fit yours. What a mess! This is what happens if we try to force-fit others into what we believe and value – no matter how reasonable that may seem to us. Examples of this follow.

- ❖ Have you ever been disappointed and unhappy when a loved one didn't phone you – and you know that in the same circumstances you would have phoned them? Here your value of consideration for others is being challenged.
- ❖ Have you ever discovered that someone you care about does not have the same view of honesty as you have and that they fiddle their expenses or their taxes or won't pay for a bottle of wine that has been missed off the bill at the local restaurant?
- ❖ How do you respond if your family don't clean or tidy up after themselves if you place a high value on neatness and cleanliness?
- ❖ What if someone cuts you up on the motorway when you believe that people should be courteous on the road? Do you get uptight?
- ❖ On a larger scale, have you ever felt gutted when someone cheated on you or broke a confidence when you value loyalty, commitment and keeping your word?
- ❖ What happens if someone does not agree with your beliefs about religion or equal opportunities or politics? Do you dig your heels in and try to persuade them that you are right or get annoyed if they don't seem to listen to your point of view.

Now while it may seem reasonable to be upset about any or all of these things, they are things over which you have no direct control. The answer here is to find a way to let go and not to let negative feelings take over. Defending your belief or value is not the same as expecting someone else to have exactly the same beliefs as you do. Respecting that others have different values and beliefs is the starting point.

Make a list of the jelly moulds in your life – the times when you set yourself up for serial disappointment, frustration and unhappiness by expecting things from others that they never deliver. These are usually prefaced by words and phrases such as should/shouldn't, ought/ought not', etc.

....

....

....

....

....

....

....

....

....

....

Now ask yourself this question for each of them. 'How can I respect that they have a different set of values and beliefs to me and how much better would it be if I let my negative feelings go now?'

WORK BOOK

Workbook Step 4 – Values and Beliefs

Guide to using the Workbook

When you are going through this workbook, you will find some of the questions easier than others. Sometimes the answers will spring instantly to mind. Other times you may need to take time out to reflect and consider what this could mean for you.

You may find it useful to go through a checklist of the areas that could affect your happiness. When answering these questions, some of the things to consider might be how your Values and Beliefs affect:

- ❖ your relationships
- ❖ your money
- ❖ your work
- ❖ your health.

This is about how what you value and what you believe and how they affect your happiness.

A What are the **three** things that you believe about yourself that add happiness to your life?

1 ....
....
....

2 ....
....
....

3 ....
....
....

B What are the **three** things you believe about other people that make your life better and happier?

1 ....
....
....

2 ....
....
....

3 ....
....
....

C What are **three** things you believe about yourself that
make you unhappy?

1 ....
....
....

2 ....
....
....

3 ....
....
....

D What are **three** things you believe about other people
that make life difficult for you and lead to unhappiness?

1 ....
....
....

2 ....
....
....

3 ....
....
....

E What are **three** things in your life that are most important to you and which make you happy?

1 ....
....
....

2 ....
....
....

3 ....
....
....

F What are the **three** greatest factors in your life that are
the cause of unhappiness?

1 ....
....
....

2 ....
....
....

3 ....
....
....

Think hard about what you have written above. Decide now
what actions you will take to spring-clean your values and beliefs, so that they work better for you and add to your happiness.
Make sure you write them down.

Actions:

....
....
....

The Happiness Challenge for Step 4 on the
Stairway of Happiness – Values and Beliefs

THE HAPPINESS MANTRA

Your happiness state will only change if you do things differently and if you increase the number of Happiness Habits you develop. Remember it takes only 21 days to create permanent change.

In order to increase your happiness, take the Happiness Challenge. Take one of the actions that you have identified in this Workbook. Every day for 21 days, stop just thinking about making this change. Go out and do it!

Progress Chart						
Day 1	Day 2	Day 3	Day 4	Day 5	Day 6	Day 7
Day 8	Day 9	Day 10	Day 11	Day 12	Day 13	Day 14
Day 15	Day 16	Day 17	Day 18	Day 19	Day 20	Day 21

New habit to be developed

....
....
....

Keep a check on your progress. Put a tick in the box every day for 21 days when you have practised that habit.

Start date ....

7

Identity - Be Yourself

The Fifth Step on the Stairway of Happiness

Here is the place to find out who you *really* are and what makes you so unique and special.

Remember! To make lasting changes to what you don't know about your Identity, you may need to work at least one Step above on the Stairway of Happiness. In other words, you need to understand more about your Purpose or direction in life.

Step 6 – Purpose
Purpose is what brings meaning into your life. It's why you are here.

Step 5 – Identity
Identity is about acknowledging your roots and accepting yourself for who you are.

Step 4 – Values and Beliefs
Values and Beliefs are the programming, power, motivation and energy behind your actions.

Step 3 – Skills and Capabilities
Skills and Capabilities are all the talents you have or could have, given the opportunity.

Step 2 – Behaviour
Behaviour includes what you do, how you do it, who you do it with and how others behave with you. It's also about what you think, what you say and how you say it.

Step 1 – Surroundings
Your Surroundings are everything you see, hear and feel when you look around you. It's your environment and the results you are getting.

Identity

As a happy person you will know yourself inside and out and accept who you are. You will know your strengths and also the areas that let you down.

Being able to be yourself springs from a certainty and an acceptance about the essence of you. Your Identity is not affected by the labels other people might want to attach to you. Part of who you are lies in your roots – your name, your country, your genes, your upbringing, your loyalties, your country of origin, your faith, the colour of your skin. But it's also about recognising that you are more than that. It's an acceptance that there are many things about yourself that you can't change, and an acknowledgement that you do not have to be imprisoned by them. You can make the most of who you are. The key to being comfortable about your Identity is recognising the qualities you have within you that make you different and unique.

Look around you. How can you be happy …

- ❖ if you are unsure of who you are
- ❖ if you are living life according to someone else's view of you
- ❖ if you have lost track of what matters to you
- ❖ if you no longer recognise who you are
- ❖ if you don't like or value yourself
- ❖ if you do not accept who you are
- ❖ if you are not being the best of who you are?

HAPPY THOUGHT

The way you see yourself and the way you feel about yourself affect what you believe to be true about yourself.

The Happiness Habit for you

You are now growing in your Happiness Habits if you have already worked out where you need to be (Surroundings), how you need to behave (Behaviour), where your real gifts lie (Skills and Capabilities) and what is important to you (Values and Beliefs). Alternatively, Identity may be your starting point and in one sense it is *the* starting point because knowing and valuing who we are is the foundation for lasting change on all of the other Steps on the Stairway of Happiness. We're talking here about self-worth – the value you place on yourself as a human being.

Do you sometimes feel that you don't know who you really are? Do you find yourself being the person that other people think you are? Being yourself springs from a certainty and knowledge about the essence of you. It is not affected by the labels other people might want to attach to you.

A happy person knows themselves inside and out and is content. Identity is about becoming more of who you already are. It is about becoming the best of who you are and developing your Identity so it is strong, clear, identifiable to others as well as to yourself. Identity is also about differentiating your role in life from who you are. Sometimes it is easy to confuse the two so one gets lost in the other. It is possible have many roles simultaneously so, for example, you can be a wife, a mother, a daughter, a carer, a teacher, and a musician without any conflict. Unhappiness can be the result of losing the balance and allowing one piece of who you are to disappear because the other aspects of your Identity absorb too much time.

Developing your Identity

We are all unique and individual. Identical twins may look alike but their personalities are different. When you look at your passport or your driving licence, it confirms who you are. It is an Identity Card with a unique number or code that belongs to you. What it does not do is give any idea about the complexity of you as a human being. The fifth Step on the Stairway of Happiness is to work out how to tap into that complexity and unravel the roots of the real you.

Some people take time out to discover more about themselves and who they really are, whether it's going on a gap year, coming off the work treadmill – at least for a spell, or starting off on a personal development journey.

HAPPY THOUGHT

Developing your uniqueness will make you attractive to other people and make you feel good about yourself.
(Larry Thompson, Hollywood Producer and manager to the stars)

Think of your Identity as fingerprints. You know that your fingerprints are unique. It's scientifically proven that they don't change over a person's lifetime. It is also a fact that no two of your fingerprints are the same. You don't just have one fingerprint, you have ten. It's the same with your Identity. There may be a number of different parts to your Identity – and they are all different parts of your uniqueness. Your fingers will grow and change over time, but the Identity print remains the same.

Sometimes people think that in order to have an Identity, they need to act the same way with different people in different situations. Identity is, however, not a prison or a cage that we cannot escape from, it is simply a foundation on which to build your life. It's your starting point. Flexibility and knowing how to act in different situations are the keys to bringing out the best of who you are.

James

James was 27 and he was struggling to know himself. He felt he was full of contradictions and therefore he was confused about what sort of a person he really was. He told us, 'I don't understand it. Sometimes I'm very shy and sometimes I'm the life and soul of the party. Sometimes I'm really patient and at other times

I am easily irritated and annoyed. There are times when I love being adventurous and taking risks, and at other times I just want to be safe and secure.' James was worried about being inconsistent at best and schizophrenic at worst.

What James didn't realise was that this is normal. By using the many parts of our personalities we ensure variety, sparkle and interest. We are not one-dimensional cardboard cut-outs. Some parts of our personality might show themselves more often than others; we might like some aspects of our personalities better than others, but they are all part of us. Once James realised that 'inconsistency' was simply a reflection of the wonderful richness of his Identity then he relaxed and felt much happier. He was then in a better position to choose which aspects of his Identity he wanted to develop most. By doing this he is on his way to becoming the best of who he is. He now has much more confidence in his life and feels good about himself.

Easily spotted

At a very early age most of us were put into school uniforms. We all stood in the Assembly Hall wearing the same tie, the same shirt, the same jumper and the same colours. Walking in the street before and after school it was easy to see where children belonged. They had a clear Identity as pupils of one school or another. On leaving school they suddenly become individuals and have to work out where they belong. Some jobs bring with them a uniform but others don't. You now have to display your Identity in a different way.

Manufacturers spend a fortune developing brands. They spend money on logos, packaging and advertising so that the Identity of their product is clearly seen and readily identifiable. Why do we buy well-known brands? Because we know what we're getting. Their Identity is on the label and we assume that certain things about that product are true. It would be surprising and disappointing if we bought a Porsche and inside it had a Lada engine – or if we bought a tin labelled peas and inside were mushrooms.

How do you display your Identity? Is it how you really are or is it a false label (or set of labels) that you have allowed someone else to stick on you?

The football scarf

Football clubs have thousands of fans, people who go to football grounds to watch their teams play or watch them on television. The performance of the team is a matter of huge importance. People often use the team that they support as a way of identifying themselves. They have a sense of belonging when they wear the scarf and the replica shirt. This Identity works well for them until the team loses a match or plays badly. Most fans are unhappy, despondent and feel miserable. Their Identity is tied up with the successes or failures of the team.

Clubs and societies

It is great to belong to clubs and societies, as it's another way of establishing clearly who we are. Whether it is the local gym, the Caravan Club, the Croquet Club, the Cricket Club, the Women's Institute, a Political Party or the Alumni Association, a membership card is part of the Identity we are seeking to establish.

Beating yourself up

How many times a day, a week, a year do you beat yourself up mentally? This happens for many people when they do something silly, don't do well at something, or when they let someone they care about down. Typically they will say things to themselves that are expressed in Identity language. These can be statements such as, 'I'm stupid', 'I'm a failure', 'I'm not a good person', 'I'm hopeless', and so on. Have you ever done that and felt the bad feelings that result?

The problem here is that you are taking one aspect of your behaviour (Step 2 on the Stairway of Happiness) and treating it as if it's your Identity (Step 5). In other words you're placing far more importance on that event or that behaviour than it merits.

To bring the situation back into perspective, simply rephrase the event in Behaviour language, for example, 'I did a stupid thing', 'I did not succeed this time', 'I did something I'm not proud of but I'm still an OK person'. This will help you take some of the emotional charge out of the situation and therefore not sabotage your emotional happiness.

Losing your Identity

Life is easy when you are given a printed business card. You can present it to people and it tells others clearly who you are. 'Jonathan McIntosh, Sales Manager, Morebrite Ltd'. Your Identity is now spelt out for all to see. When redundancy strikes or you lose your job, however, the business card is taken away and you suddenly have to describe yourself in another way. People who give up work to look after their children full time or to care for aged relatives have the same quandary in describing themselves. They often feel that they are worth less now that they are no longer an Engineer, a Production Manager, an Accountant, a Marketing Manager, a Social Worker or a Sales Person. They realise that conversations with new acquaintances usually begin with, 'And what do you do?' A common difficulty therefore for these people then is overcoming the blow to self-esteem and the ensuing unhappiness that comes from this insecurity.

HAPPY THOUGHT
You are not what you do, you are not your job, you are not your
role, you are not your emotions, you are not your thoughts.
You are yourself.

Friends Reunited

The website www.friendsreunited.co.uk is dedicated to finding old friends, getting back in touch with them and organising re-unions. It has had stunning success, allowing people who had lost touch to find each other again, to talk over old times and to discover what people are doing now. Everyone seems to want to go back in time and see themselves in the context of their school life. Why does it have such a fascination? Partly it is curiosity to see what other people have done with their lives and partly it is to see yourself in the context of who you used to be. You hear from others what they thought of you then and you have the opportunity to do the same. You can show people who you are now and what you have become. This website and the connections that come from it tap into your need to establish your Identity. School friends know who you were and saw you every day for years. Connecting with them again later in life allows you to revisit yourself, seeing yourself as others saw you.

Genes Reunited

The success of Friends Reunited was followed by that of www.genesreunited.co.uk, the website that enables people to trace their roots either because they have a keen genealogical hobby or because they have a need to trace relatives they have lost. Again, people want to find out where they belong. They need to know who they are, who their parents are and where they have come from. They want to understand their roots as this will allow them to know more about who they are.

Genetic links

Clare Short, the Ladywood MP, gave up a baby up for adoption in the mid 1960s when she was a student. Just over 31 years after the event, her son decided to trace his birth mother – Ms Short having notified the adoption agency that she wanted to be contacted if ever her child desired it.

Toby Graham, staunch Tory and City lawyer, found himself with Clare Short MP as a mother.

The media images of them hugging are some of the most heart-warming of recent political history. Clare Short was not only found by her son, she also learnt that she was a grand-mother.

The identity crisis

Sometimes we just don't know who we are. We have a sudden crisis of thinking that calls into question what we are doing and who we are doing it with. Occasionally it is triggered by age, such as reaching a landmark birthday of 20, 40 or 60 – but it can happen at any time. Perhaps we wonder if we were meant to be doing the job we are doing or if we have spent our lives so far ignoring a part of us that could be doing something more exciting. This worry and uncertainty leads to unhappiness and can only be resolved by looking at the Step above, Purpose. By identifying what part in the world we want to play, we will have to address who we are and how we can make the most of our lives.

Being yourself

Sometimes we feel it is difficult to be ourselves. We feel that if we show others who we really are, they will not like us or approve of us.

Sue

Sue, an Anglican priest, struggled with the fact that she held strong religious beliefs as well as being a committed feminist. She said that when she was with her like-minded religious friends she felt she had to hide her feminism and when she was with her feminist friends she felt she had to deny her religious beliefs. As a consequence she felt uncomfortable and did not think that she was being true to herself. The resulting internal conflict and the feeling that she was being deceitful led to great unhappiness. She assumed that who she was would be unacceptable to others and thought she knew what others wanted her to be. When she decided to be upfront about her beliefs, she discovered that no one really cared about them and in fact had suspected that this was the case all along. The problem existed in Sue's mind, not in reality.

Denying who you are leads to unhappiness and dissatisfaction.

Reducing negative feelings

Negative feelings such as guilt or anger or frustration or fear are often the result of conflict between what psychologists call our actual self and our ideal self. We do not always live up to the best that we are capable of being. This sets off an internal conflict between what we have actually done (or not done), been (or not been) on the one hand and what we feel *should* have happened on the other. These self-imposed rules often serve little purpose and add unnecessary unhappiness to our lives.

Age and who you are

Some people just don't want to be old. They want to retain the zest of youth as well as the appearance. Others settle comfortably for who they are. Part of your Identity is what you look like. You look in the mirror and you know who you are. Others look at you and recognise you even if they have not seen you for years.

A recent survey shows that more than one in ten British women have had cosmetic surgery, as going under-the-knife becomes as normal as wearing make-up or highlighting their hair. A further 54% say they will have it in the future after being inspired by the 'nips-and-tucks' of stars like Demi Moore and Anne Robinson. An overwhelming 96% of British women 'constantly worry about their body shape and size', 83% 'don't think they have a good body' and 81% say their body 'makes them feel down'.

It would seem that if your reflection in the mirror is out of synch with your Identity, then the 21st-century person has the chance to do something about it. Changing your body image may help your self-esteem but it cannot entirely replace any lack of value you place on yourself as a person. It could also be worthwhile, therefore, to work on other ways to feel good about who you are.

Fighting the failure demon

It's surprising how many people restrict the amount of happiness in their lives by allowing feelings of failure to flood what they do. These feelings are rather like the undertow that pulls a swimmer away from the safety of the warm waters close to the shore and out into cold and dangerous territory.

Accepting that you don't have to do great things in order to be a great person is the best starting point here. Ironically, if you believe you are great, you are actually more likely to do great things!

HAPPY THOUGHT
You don't have to do great things in order to be a great person.

Identity theft

It is deeply unsettling and worrying when you discover that someone has stolen your Identity. The first clue is when you open your credit card statement and you spot strange and expensive transactions. The realisation slowly dawns that someone has cloned your credit card and is going around acting as if they were you. They are spending money with a card that bears your name. You now have to trawl though all of the transactions, working out which ones were from the real you and which ones from the person who pretended to be you. What did this person look like? How did they behave? How troubling it is to know that someone wants to take over your Identity and be you.

Nature or nature?

There are some aspects of our Identity that we may have little or no choice about. We can't choose our parents, our race, the place where we are born, or our genetic make-up. These are our Identity 'fingerprints', the indelible and unchanging parts of who we are. There are, however, choices we can make about other aspects of our Identity. As we go through life we can grow as people, just as our fingers, hands, hair, nails and bodies grow. We are different as adults to the way we were as children, but we still have the same basic Identity. A liberating thought is that we can choose how we feel about the various cards we have been dealt in life. We can choose many of the roles we have; we can develop or ignore what nature and nurture gave us – for good or ill. Our first Brilliant Idea looks at this and gives you the chance to explore who you are from the roots up.

HAPPY THOUGHT

Heather says, 'I'm glad my name is Summers. If I had been called Winters, I would have found that much harder to relate to as I see myself as a sunshine person'.

Brilliant Ideas to develop the Happiness Habit in your Identity

1 Identity parade

How does our Identity develop over time? This happens as a result of a number of factors – some of which we have control over and some of which we don't. Various aspects of Identity are shown in the Identity Parade Chart below. Inspect each of them in turn and give them a rating on a scale of 1–10 where 10 is very happy about that aspect of your Identity and 1 is not at all happy. This will give you some clues as to which aspects of your Identity you can feel good about and what new or different choices you can make about areas you are not so happy with. If there is simply nothing you can do to change something, then decide how you could look at that aspect of your Identity more positively.

The Identity Parade

Ways in which our Identity can develop over time	Amount of choice we have
Our genetic make-up Our genes determine what we look like and who we look like, how tall we can grow, the colour of our skin and our hair and the sort of talents and skills that come to us naturally, e.g. how fast we can run, how musical we are, how good we are with our hands, how healthy we are, whether we are naturally placid or aggressive. How happy are you with your genetic make-up? *Rating 1–10* _____	We have no choice over our genetic make-up. Our genes may determine the maximum height we can grow to, but our diet and our environment may mean that we never actually reach that height. (Scientists tell us that environment can make as much as 20 cm difference to someone's height.) Similar principles apply to our weight. We may be naturally a certain shape and weight, but our lifestyle and diet may make us heavier or lighter. We may never have had opportunities presented to us to help us explore and develop all the talents and potential that we have. However, these talents are still within us – perhaps waiting for a time when we choose to find out more of what we are capable of becoming. We have many choices over the cosmetic aspects of our Identity – such as hair colour, how we dress, etc. – and they are usually a direct result of how we feel about ourselves.

153

Ways in which our Identity can develop over time	Amount of choice we have
Our race, colour and culture We inherit this aspect of our Identity. We are born to parents of particular nationalities, we are born in a particular country and our passports declare both our country of origin and our place of birth. If we identify with them, we are likely to adopt many of the values, traditions and religious beliefs (or lack of them) that are passed down the generations. The place and the house we are brought up in are beyond our control. The environment we lived in as a child will give us our regional loyalties, our regional accents and our feeling of where we belong in society How happy are you with your race / colour / culture? *Rating 1–10* _____	It is not possible to change the colour of our skin – nor the nationality of our natural parents. We have, however, the choice to identify with our nationality / or race – and be proud of it. This is likely to give us strong roots and a feeling of belonging that will stand us in good stead in our lives. If we have been brought up within a particular culture, faith or creed we may have had no choice but to conform when young, yet it is likely to have had a significant impact on how we feel about ourselves. Depending on how they are preached, religions can offer their followers everything from fantastic self-belief, support and a road to happiness on the one hand to feelings of unworthiness, guilt and fear on the other. Every adult now has significant choice about which traditions or creeds to accept or reject. We can choose which aspects of our heritage we want to keep and which to reject. Taking the best from our childhood environment and choosing whether to be restricted by it or not will have a high impact on how we live our lives and how happy we are.

154

Ways in which our Identity can develop over time	Amount of choice we have
Our names One of the earliest questions we are asked as children is 'What's your name?' Our names are *given* to us when we are born. Names are therefore a key part of our Identity. They are the first thing we present to others to tell them a little bit about who we are. How happy are you with your name(s)? *Rating 1–10* _____	Some people like their names, others are neutral about them, a few people are embarrassed about them and others hate their names. How you feel about your name affects how you feel about yourself and therefore affects your happiness. This is so important that many people change their names – not just to 'stage' names but to ones that make them feel better about themselves. More and more women are choosing whether to take on their husband or partner's name depending on whether or not it 'fits' with who they are as a person. Remember too that names are often connected with race and country of origin, so how we feel about one may affect the other. Keeping or changing your name is a choice that everyone has.

Ways in which our Identity can develop over time	Amount of choice we have
Our upbringing and experiences The way we were brought up, has a major impact on our feelings towards ourselves and how worthwhile we are as people. How we were treated (especially when young) by our parents, brothers / sisters, friends, schoolmates, teachers and other significant adults around us often has a lasting effect on people for the rest of our lives. How happy are you with your upbringing? *Rating 1–10* _____	Some people are very fortunate and have had an upbringing that was loving, supportive and encouraging. Others are less fortunate. Many children are abused, unloved, neglected, or bullied and carry the mental and physical scars. The bad news here is that some of them go on to become like the people who treated them badly. Others carry the feelings of unworthiness with them well into adulthood and sometimes for the rest of their lives. They somehow allow the past to dictate the future. The good news is that many more learn from these experiences, find ways to forgive the people who hurt them and have let go of the bad experiences in the past, choosing to create their own happy futures. Of course your experiences as an adult may also affect your self-esteem and therefore your happiness. The thing to remember here is that your experiences are not you. You can choose to accept them as defining part of who you are – or you can choose to view them as something separate and not part of your Identity.

Ways in which our Identity can develop over time	Amount of choice we have
What other people tell us about ourselves (our labels) Especially as children – but also as adults – we can take on board what other people tell us about ourselves. We assume that what they say about who we are is true and this affects our picture of how we see ourselves. The way we describe ourselves is also a label. Whenever we say, 'I am …' followed by a description of ourselves, we are labelling ourselves. These labels can work for us or against us. If we treat them as true, we will act in accordance with those labels whether they are good for us or not. How happy are you about how other people label you and how you label yourself? *Rating 1–10* _____	The trick here is to begin to separate out what others tell us – or have told us – about ourselves that is really true, from what isn't. Consider all the things that people said when you were little that began with the words, 'You are …'. Make two columns, one with a positive heading and the other with a negative heading. Which has more in it? These are very powerful Identity labels. Now add in the, 'You are …' things that people have said/still say about you now, as an adult. Of course you cannot change what people said in the past, but you can choose to keep them on your list or to strike them off now. Similarly you can accept or challenge the labels people give you now. For example If someone says, 'You are unkind', you can reply something like, 'I don't accept that I am an unkind person. I may sometimes unwittingly do things that are unkind but this does not make me unkind.' Remember that it's just as important here to be very careful what you say to yourself and how you label yourself repeatedly. If you are in the habit of saying negative things to yourself such as, 'You're so stupid' or 'I am a failure', you are affecting your Identity and damaging your self-esteem and therefore your happiness. It is far better to express things at the Behaviour level on the Stairway of Happiness – for example, 'I did a stupid thing' or 'That was not a success.'

2 Role-stripping

Write down a list of all the roles you have in your life. Cover everything you can think of – from parent to son/daughter to cook/gardener/listener/mediator and so on. Once you have finished your list, look at it and say to yourself, 'Whatever roles I play in my life I am also more than that.'

3 I am

Take a sheet of paper with a plus and minus at the top as shown below. Write a list of your attributes – both positive and negative – the things that describe who you are as a person. If you find yourself putting more on the negative side, then stop! Make sure your positive side keeps up. Remember you may even find that the same attribute goes down on both sides of the sheet.

+	−

4 Other people's negative labels

Think of the labels you have been given by others throughout your life – both positive and negative. Are they true? If you believe them, then you are likely to act upon them as if they were true. So decide now if they are *really* true or whether or not they are adding to your happiness or taking away from it.

Which labels will you keep and which ones will you choose to throw away?

Labels	*Really* true?	Does this help or hinder my happiness?

Now, look at the list again and add in what could be true if you tried it out. Remember whatever you think you are, you are more than that.

To grow the Happiness Habit, choose one thing you have never done before, something you always assumed you could not do and do it. This will release unexpected trapped creativity.

5 Your business card

The next time somehow asks who you are, be ready for them with a true answer. Instead of fobbing them off, be ready with a well thought through reply. Fill in the box below. Do it several times and have a few answers ready that begin to explore the depths of the real you.

6 The elevator speech

Prepare a speech to describe yourself to a complete stranger that you meet in a lift. Be able to give a concise description of who you are in such a way that your new companion has a crystal clear view of your Identity. You need to be able to do this in the time that it takes the lift to travel from the ground to the first floor.

7 Building your confidence

A lot of self-confidence is related directly to self-worth. The higher your self-worth, the higher your confidence. Many people who suffer from low confidence put themselves down. When things go wrong, they translate the event to the Identity Step on the Stairway of Happiness instead of recognising that it's on the Behaviour Step. This makes them feel bad about themselves rather than working out what they can do about their behaviour. Confidence relates to your perceived level of ability in the things you want to be good at. If you are looking for perfection, you will be constantly disappointed and unhappy. If you are over-competitive and feel unhappy every time you don't win or do your best, you're likely to orchestrate your own unhappiness. How can you stop this and build your confidence?

Try this.

Make a list of the times and events when you regularly expect too much from yourself, when you expect to be perfect, or to win

For each item on your list, ask yourself the question, 'How can I make learning and not perfection my goal? What can I learn?' Focus on that and enjoy developing your skills.

WORK BOOK

Workbook Step 5 - Identity

Guide to using the Workbook

When you are going through this Workbook, you will find some of the questions easier than others. Sometimes the answers will spring instantly to mind. Other times you may need to take time out to reflect and consider what this could mean for you.

You may find it useful to go through a checklist of the areas that could affect your happiness. When answering these questions, some of the things you think about with regard to your Identity could be:

- ❖ you and your relationships
- ❖ you and your money
- ❖ you and your work
- ❖ you and your health.

This is about gaining a picture of who you really are, rather than living your life according to how others might see you.

A What three **things** do you know to be true about yourself that help you day to day and add to your happiness?

1 ....
....
....

2 ....
....
....

3 ....
....
....

B What **three** things do people say you are that help you
to be happy?

1 ....
....
....

2 ....
....
....

3 ....
....
....

C What labels do people put on you that prevent you
from being as happy as you might be?

1 ....
....
....

2 ....
....
....

3 ....
....
....

D What three things do you know about yourself that make life difficult for you and perhaps lead to unhappiness?

1 ....
   ....
   ....

2 ....
   ....
   ....

3 ....
   ....
   ....

Think hard about what you have written above. Decide now what actions you will take to be more true to your real self and, therefore, add to your happiness. Make sure you write them down.

Actions:

   ....
   ....
   ....

The Happiness Challenge for Step 5 on the Stairway of Happiness - Identity

THE HAPPINESS MANTRA

Your happiness state will only change if you do things differently and if you increase the number of Happiness Habits you develop. Remember it takes only 21 days to create permanent change.

In order to increase your happiness, take the Happiness Challenge.

Take one of the actions that you have identified in this Workbook. Every day for 21 days, stop just thinking about making this change. Go out and do it!

New habit to be developed

....

....

....

Keep a check on your progress. Put a tick in the box every day for 21 days when you have practised that habit.

Progress Chart						
Day 1	Day 2	Day 3	Day 4	Day 5	Day 6	Day 7
Day 8	Day 9	Day 10	Day 11	Day 12	Day 13	Day 14
Day 15	Day 16	Day 17	Day 18	Day 19	Day 20	Day 21

Start date ....

8

Purpose

The Sixth Step on the Stairway of Happiness

This is the top Step on the Stairway of Happiness. It is the most powerful of all the levels as it affects all the Steps below. Being clearer about your Purpose will help you set your life's course in the best possible direction. This will provide you with the energy and the motivation to stay on that path so that you can achieve the most from your life and therefore experience maximum happiness

Because Purpose is at the top of the Stairway of Happiness, it is the key to lasting change on all the other Steps. There is therefore no higher Step to which you can go that can affect or change your Purpose. It's simply a matter of discovering more about what's already there. At this level it's good to be aware of your place in the grand scheme of things, to know that you are part of a bigger picture, that you have a right to be there and that you have a valid contribution to make.

Step 6 – Purpose
Purpose is what brings meaning into your life. It's why you are here.

Step 5 – Identity
Identity is about acknowledging your roots and accepting yourself for who you are.

Step 4 – Values and Beliefs
Values and Beliefs are the programming, power, motivation and energy behind your actions.

Step 3 – Skills and Capabilities
Skills and Capabilities are all the talents you have or could have, given the opportunity.

Step 2 – Behaviour
Behaviour includes what you do, how you do it, who you do it with and how others behave with you. It's also about what you think, what you say and how you say it.

Step 1 – Surroundings
Your Surroundings are everything you see, hear and feel when you look around you. It's your environment and the results you are getting.

Purpose

Purpose is what brings meaning into your life and the recognition that you are part of a larger whole. It answers the big life question 'Why am I here?' Some people are born with a conviction about the sort of vocation they would like to follow. They have a calling in life and this gives them a personal life map that provides them with a strong direction. If you have a clear sense of Purpose, you are likely to be happy and successfully integrate

> your dreams into your life. Those who lack Purpose can find they
> are restless, aimless or feel dissatisfied with their lives.

Look around you. How can you be happy ...

- ❖ if you feel that you are wandering aimlessly through life
- ❖ if you have no dreams
- ❖ if life seems to have little meaning
- ❖ if there is no higher power or system that you can connect to or with?

We have now arrived at the top Step of the Stairway of Happiness – Purpose. Some of you begin life here. You have total clarity about your ultimate Purpose in life. As a consequence of this you know who you are; you are clear about what is important to you in life and what you believe in. You are confident about what you are able to do and achieve. You are also comfortable with where you are.

Others have different starting points on the Stairway of Happiness. It may be that you started on Step 1 where you needed to sort out your Surroundings first and foremost, eliminating those factors in your environment that were preventing you from moving up the Stairway.

Where you start is neither good nor bad. It depends on factors such as where you were born, what circumstances you were born into, what genes you inherited and what opportunities naturally came your way. The good news is that the Stairway is open to everyone. If you stand on a Step and you don't move, however, you will be there forever. Staying in the same spot will not allow you the opportunity to change the things you don't want in your life or increase the things that will bring you happiness.

Purpose is what gives life meaning. It's knowing that you are here for a reason; it's having a sense of what you want and don't want in life. It's then using that knowledge and those instincts to define your path through life.

Our ultimate Purpose as human beings is to achieve happiness. The dilemma is to work out the route to take and to recognise happiness when you have found it. If you don't have a map, you are less likely to get to your destination than if you do. Happiness means different things to different people. It's the feel-good factor – feeling good about yourself and other people.

Within Purpose, the top Step of the Staircase of Happiness, there are 4 levels that we operate at.

Level 1 – Busyness. Unfocused activity and lots of it (headless chicken/busy fool).
Level 2 – Structure. Focused repetitive/routine, 'legitimate' activity, e.g. work/sport (golf on Sunday, tea and cakes on Friday).
Level 3 – Goal and dreams. Activities that provide life with real meaning and motivate us to do more/do better, etc.
Level 4 – Spirituality or Higher Purpose – the ultimate in meaning and happiness, making life truly worthwhile. Improving the human condition, developing the human spirit.

Levels 1 and 2, the shaded areas, are commonly mistaken for Purpose but in practice are probably false. Level 3 is more nearly attuned to real Purpose and provides increased opportunity for true, meaningful and lasting happiness. Level 4 is true Purpose. In the 21st century, subscribing to this level has not been fashionable until recently. However, there is a groundswell building up as people search for meaning in our increasingly commercial and materialistic world. Money and success, and all the trappings they bring, are somehow not enough for many people. They are searching for more meaning and purpose than just materialistic success.

Level 1 – Busyness

This is the lowest level within Step 6 – Purpose. In reality it is a false aspect of Purpose. It's what happens if you do not have structure, goals, vision or spirituality in your life. We're talking here about the treadmill, excess and sometimes unnecessary busyness.

Busyness often replaces true Purpose for people who are not at that point in their lives where they are prepared to face up to some of the issues, barriers, or painful experiences in their lives. They rush around, cramming every minute of their lives with busyness and activity. This means that they do not have the time to think about the things they would rather not face. The busyness is an unconscious safety mechanism that acts as a smoke screen or a protection from feelings of pain or unhappiness. It also provides some sense of meaning or Purpose in your life.

Another common reason for this kind of excess busyness is simply survival. People who live in circumstances where they need to provide for their family, or to save a failing business and keep their heads above water financially are concerned with getting through each day. They are likely to fall into bed exhausted every night and find it hard to get out of bed in the morning. Again there is simply not time to focus on the bigger issues of life. Feelings of meaning and Purpose are derived not from the activities themselves but from knowing that they have prevented disaster or that they have not gone under.

This level of Purpose and meaning is made up of many small actions, with no real focus or direction.

Level 2 – Structure

This level of Purpose is made up of larger chunks of activity. In this case the activities have more innate value and can bring pleasure. This might range from having a challenging and satisfying job, to regular treats such as having a meal out every Friday. Regularity, routine and habit and security are the key aspects here. Comfort and feelings of worthwhileness come from the repetition and familiarity of a key set of activities engaged in. There is a structure to the day, the week, the year. Things have their place and there is logic to them. Somehow they fit together and provide direction and meaning to the way that someone spends their time.

The feelings of satisfaction or happiness at this level are likely to be greater than those in Level 1, but for many people the structure loses its appeal and can become meaningless after some time. Routine becomes empty or just boring and meaning-less repetition.

Level 3 – Vision and goals

This is a higher level of Purpose. Those operating at this level are inspired by a personal vision or set of life goals. These may be for themselves or for society at large. Achieving them brings a great deal of happiness and satisfaction that is lasting. For some people, the dream is something they have always known. They haven't had to sit down and work out what it is that will drive them and give their lives meaning. Others will approach this more consciously. They will write down or be able to describe their mission in life clearly because they have thought it through. They are likely to have clear goals which are written down and amended in the light of experience. Most of their actions will automatically be directed towards their overall goals.

Level 4 – Higher Purpose or Spirituality

This is the highest level of Purpose and is about our spirituality as human beings. It takes different forms. Spirituality may mean a religion or a belief in God or some higher being whether it's Christianity, Buddhism, or something else. For others who may have no specific religion, it is a sense that there is something greater out there and that we are all part of a larger plan. It can be called many things – Higher Purpose, the Collective Consciousness, the Wisdom of the Universe, etc. Those who come to this way of thinking or feeling achieve lasting happiness in their lives. It arises from a sense that they are contributing to the development of the universe or the improvement of the human race. They have a place and a Purpose in the grand scheme of things.

Being highly spiritual does not mean having your head in the clouds or sitting meditating at the top of a mountain (although of course it can do!). It can have a very practical application that shows itself in having the sort of goals and dreams described at Level 3 that are placed within this wider context and which lead towards your overall Purpose in life.

Viktor Frankl was a survivor of the Holocaust who spent five years in Auschwitz and other concentration camps. He lost everything there and he had nothing to call his own. What meaning or Purpose in his life kept him going and how did he find the will to survive? He says in his book, *Man's Search for Meaning* that he believes that man's deepest desire is to search for meaning and Purpose. No one could take away his imagination and his vision of himself as a part of a greater Purpose. He said that, 'Our generation is realistic, for we have come to know man as he really is. After all, man is that being who invented the gas chambers of Auschwitz; however, he is also that being who entered those gas chambers upright, with the Lord's Prayer or the Shema Yisrael on his lips.'

Knowing your Purpose

Some lucky people have always known what they want out of life. They have a natural vocation or calling in life and know they want to be a doctor, a nurse, a vet, an entrepreneur, a member of the clergy, a teacher, a parent, a pilot, a train driver, a journalist, a poet, an artist, a musician, or a sportsperson. These people are in the minority. Most of us keep looking and keep hoping that what we want to do will spring out of our current activities. Very few students going off to university know what they are going to do when they leave.

Many people spend the majority of their lives at work. If they are lucky they get a couple of months' holiday period, weekends free and the rest of the year they travel to and from work, think about work, anticipate or worry about work. If you have a vocation, it's easier to remain focused and motivated. But what about those who find work a bit of a drudge? Many of us go to work as a routine, because we have to. We don't get any real pleasure from it. The motivation can be that the salary 'pays the bills' or sometimes people just enjoy their colleagues and friends at work but dislike what they do, are bored by the job and just plod through the working day.

Happy people have got the magic formula known as work/life balance. They derive as much pleasure from life at home as they do from life at work. Unhappy people are those who have got the balance wrong.

It's not necessarily important to be able to say or to write down what your Purpose in life is. What is important is staying tuned in to what feels right and good for you. This is the true road to happiness.

A wife and mother

For as long as Martha could remember, all she wanted to do was to be a wife and mother. She married George who also wished to have a big family. They brought up four children, who each found their own way in life and eventually left home.

The eldest, Rachel, qualified as a physiotherapist and lives 200 miles away in London. Richard went to Australia and became manager of a hotel in Sydney. Ros graduated in languages and went to Brussels to work in the European Parliament. Charles, the youngest, was the export sales manager for a distillery and travelled the world. He was seldom at home.

What had brought meaning to Martha's life were her children. When they left, she felt empty and bewildered. Life no longer had meaning. After months of loneliness and misery, she realised her Purpose in life, being a mother, had gone. She began asking herself how else she could fulfil her Purpose and take on a mother's role. She remembered how happy she had been when looking after her children when they were small and she started looking round outside her tight family circle to see if she could do something useful. Martha now works as a volunteer in a school three days a week. She loves every minute of it and she feels valued, useful and happy.

The paradox of success

To illustrate how important Purpose is, think about what happens when people achieve the things that they mistakenly think will bring them happiness. Typically the thinking goes something like this.

- ❖ When I'm grown up, I'll be happy.
- ❖ When I'm married, I'll be happy.
- ❖ When I have children I'll be happy.

❖ When I'm rich I'll be happy – and so on.

In these cases, you are treating happiness as something outside yourself and therefore outside your control. While achieving each of those goals may bring some degree of happiness with them, there is no guarantee that they will bring long-term satisfaction unless they are in line with your sense of Purpose.

You can have happiness any time, any place, anywhere.

Happiness is a state, a mood, a feeling. This means you don't have to wait for it – or leave it to chance. You can have happiness now. It's within you. It's much easier to believe this and to control your own happiness if you feel you're playing a worthwhile part in the destiny of the universe.

Many people who have achieved their goal of becoming rich or famous or successful find that achieving these goals does not give them all the happiness and satisfaction they anticipated. They start looking for a deeper meaning in life. Some of them get involved in charities, others look to religion or spirituality to provide more meaning. Having a deeper Purpose brings them increased motivation energy and ultimately happiness.

Not many of us sit down and contemplate our sense of Purpose. The process of discovering our Purpose tends to be more instinctive and intuitive.

We build structure into our lives to give meaning to our day-to-day activities. We do this through the work that we do and through our daily habits and our routines. These give us a sense of Purpose even although it may be superficial. It's only when these routines become boring, irritating, mundane or meaningless that feelings of dissatisfaction are likely to build up. If this has ever happened to you, it's likely that you began asking yourself questions such as:

❖ Is this how it's meant to be?
❖ Is this all there is?
❖ Is this what life's about?

- ❖ Isn't there more to life than this?
- ❖ Have I made a difference?
- ❖ Why am I here?

These questions may also be triggered by major traumatic life events that get us to question the meaning of life. Just think of all the stories you read in the newspapers about people who have suffered the loss of a loved one under difficult circumstances. This loss has caused them to re-examine their Purpose in life. Many of them have discovered true Purpose through founding or supporting charities related to their loss. One well-known example of this was the murder of estate agent Suzy Lamplugh. Her mother began and still runs the Suzy Lamplugh Trust with a mission to minimise the damage caused to individuals and to society by aggression in all its forms – physical, verbal and psychological. It is now the leading authority on personal safety.

Meaning out of tragedy

Roddy Scott was a British freelance cameraman working for Britain's Frontline, a television news agency. In September 2002 he was killed in the Russian Republic of Ingushetia near the border with Chechnya, following clashes between Russian forces and a group of Chechen fighters. Roddy had gone to Georgia's Panjshir Gorge, which borders Chechnya, in June with the aim to link up with Chechen fighters. He was outstandingly brave, an adventurous and independent operator who took the kind of risks that journalists around the world take every day to cover the news. He died aged 31, leaving his parents, Stina and Robin, to grieve, their lives changed forever.

Since that terrible day in 2002, his parents have become relentless fundraisers for the Rory Peck Trust, a charity with an ongoing commitment to the welfare and safety of freelance newsgatherers. The Trust subsidises training in hostile environments, provides financial and moral support to freelancers in need, and to the families of those killed, imprisoned or seriously injured during the course of their work.

In 2005, Stina went to Afghanistan with a group organised by Sandy Gall to walk through the Panjshir Valley, raising funds for the SGAA, a charity set up to support Afghans who had lost limbs through the years of fighting in their country. Stina, Robin, their family and their friends have a renewed sense of Purpose over the last three years. They cannot change the tragedy and loss that hit their lives. What they can do is to raise funds and raise awareness so that other cameramen and reporters are better equipped when they go into remote and dangerous places. They organise auctions, hog roasts, book signings; they put themselves in arduous and difficult positions in order to keep the memory of Roddy alive and ensure that his contribution lives on through them. Their tireless efforts to raise money and to support the work of charities means that a difference has been made. To see what they are doing visit www.rorypecktrust.org

Dreams

An important aspect of having a clear Purpose in life is to have great dreams. These dreams will somehow enable us to fulfil our Purpose. We may see them as wild or impractical, but if they fit in with our feelings of Purpose, they may be just what's needed to help us get there. So just make sure that the dreams you have are the ones you've chosen for yourself and you're not spending your life fulfilling the dream someone else has or had for you. This is about finding your own Purpose in life.

Small steps are sometimes what are needed to make your dreams a reality. It does not have involve giving up everything you are doing.

She's so confident

Laura Marks is someone who has a very successful career and enjoys taking on new responsibilities and new learning. Deep inside her was a dream of writing something – to be an author or a playwright – but there was never the time or the opportunity. It was never the right moment to take such a major plunge. Then one day she read in the local paper that there was a competition to 'Write a play in Sixty Seconds'. Laura read the article again and decided to enter. She sat down and began to write it there and then and in an afternoon created a sixty-second play called *She's so confident* … Laura says she used to be a great planner and re-searcher and she astonished herself by just plunging straight in.

She won the competition and it was performed in a theatre in Brooklyn in 2005 together with 99 plays from around the world. It was broadcast digitally and Laura now realises that this is the beginning of something new. The challenge for her is to do it in a bigger way. She knows that the confidence won from a sixty-second production written in the UK and produced in New York will give her the energy to believe in her dream and her abilities to achieve it. She has a renewed sense of purpose and has created her own new path to follow. She has also learned that major change can come from one small action.

If you would like to listen to Laura's play, go to www.screamingmediaproductions.com

Your dream – not mine

Equally important is not to impose your dreams on other people. You cannot force-fit people into your picture of what you think is right for them. Just as you need the freedom to decide what is right for you, they need the freedom to decide what is right for them.

One other check to make – are you living your own life or are you living your life through someone else?

> ## Dreams and reality
>
> Catriona was a nanny. She had no formal qualifications but managed to secure a job working for a wealthy woman who had three children. The family entertained the rich and famous, went on holiday to exotic locations, shopped in expensive stores and ate in fabulous restaurants. Catriona lived her life for many years through her employer. It must be said that she was happy. Her life was very different to the council flat she had been brought up in and the life she had seemed to be the best she could have. Nonetheless, she had not found her true vocation.
>
> When the children grew older and no longer needed a nanny, Catriona's life collapsed. She intended to find another similar position. Through a series of chances and coincidences, however, Catriona discovered that she had a passion for horses and an aptitude for riding. She is now a riding instructor at a well-known riding school and her Purpose (although she might not express it this way) is to help others make the best of their riding skills. She is now a person in her own right, she is living her own dream and she is happier than she has ever been.

Stop wasting time on regrets and start looking forward

What has brought real meaning into your life so far? What are the biggest things that have brought meaning and purpose into your life to date? What has made you feel worthwhile and given you the glow that you have achieved something of note and made a real difference at some level:

1 ....

2 ....

3 ....

These should give you clues about what the ingredients are for your personal Purpose in life.

Now use this information to decide what you want the future to hold. What will you want people to say about you once you are gone?

Name the **three** things you would like people to say about what difference you made to the world.

1 ....

2 ....

3 ....

Brilliant Ideas to develop the Happiness Habit by bringing more Purpose in your life – it will only take you 21 days!

1 Realise your dreams

What do you dream about doing that you've never done?

....

What do you dream about having that you've never had?

....
....
....
....

What do you dream about being that you've never been?

....
....
....
....

Now write down some of your wildest dreams. Be reckless!
Imagine what it would be like if they were fulfilled!

....
....
....
....

Think about what you have written above. Would achieving
at least part of your wildest dream help you to answer questions such as, 'Why am I here?' and 'What's my Purpose in life?'
'Where do I fit in the grand scheme of things?' Would it give you
a feeling that your life had had more value and that you had
done something really worthwhile? If the answer to at least one
of these questions is yes, then think carefully about the dream
and what you can do to bring it into reality.

If you can imagine something, then it's possible.

Now what are you prepared to do to turn those dreams into
reality and help fulfil your Purpose in life? Select the ones that
best fit with who you are as a person, your Values and Beliefs,
your Skills and Capabilities, and then write down the first Step
you will take that will set you on the road to getting there.

2 Whose dream is it anyway?

Make sure that the dream you've chosen is your own dream and not someone else's. If you feel this is being selfish, then think again. It's more likely that it's more selfish to deny your dream. If you do that, you are not fulfilling your Purpose on earth. You are less of a person than you could be and therefore you are not showing others the way to fulfil their potential.

Write down any ways in which your own dream is being diluted because you are living your life through others.

....
....
....
....

Now write down how you intend to change.

....
....
....
....

3 Check out your language

Check through the list below and make sure that none of these apply to you. They may be versions of the sort of things that were said to you when you were little. Are you repeating them and restricting the freedom of others?

- ❖ Be a doctor just like your father.
- ❖ Be a famous footballer like I should/could have been.
- ❖ Learn to play the piano to Grade 8, as I would love to have done.
- ❖ Have children so I can have grandchildren.

- ❖ Get married before you are too old.
- ❖ Go to university and get a good degree.
- ❖ Take on the family business.
- ❖ Travel the world. I never had the chance.
- ❖ Don't get married; keep your freedom. I regret the loss of mine.
- ❖ Start your own business and take a few risks like I did.
- ❖ Get on the housing ladder early – I wish I had.
- ❖ Go to night school and learn a foreign language. We never had opportunities like that when we were young.

What unfulfilled dreams do you have that you are imposing on those around you?

....
....
....
....

How can you live your own dreams instead?

....
....
....
....

4 Getting out of bed

Ask yourself how much energy you get and give to work. Do you wake up in the morning and jump out of bed, eager to get on with the working day or are you counting the days to your next day off?

Write this down on a scale of 1 to 10, where 1 is 'little or no motivation or energy' and 10 is 'full of energy and motivation'.

If your score is below 5 you should reconsider what you are doing. What exactly is wrong with where you are? Is it the job itself, is it the people you work with, is it your daily commute, is it your boss, is it what you are paid? The first step towards the Happiness Habit is defining what is wrong and then imagining what the perfect job would look like. Now is the time to look at your talents and those qualities you have as an individual that are not being used in your daily work. What ambitions did you have as a child, a teenager or an adult that you have never fulfilled? If you can tap in to what is going on inside you with true self-awareness, then you can do what you need to do to bring it all to the surface and actively manage it in your life. There is just no point in having talents and personal qualities if you don't get on and use them. Sometimes a way of life becomes a habit and we behave in the way that we always have. We ignore our real feelings, perhaps out of habit, perhaps out of fear, and we become less than the person we could be because we are not fulfilling our Purpose in life.

❖ Think through all the previous Brilliant Ideas in this Step and write down your initial thoughts about your main purpose or direction in life.

....
....
....

5 How to get started

A lack of Purpose often shows itself in a lack of motivation. It may be that you find you need someone else to prompt you to do something before you can launch into action or to finish off a task or project. It may be that instead of doing what you know to be urgent and important, you find yourself doing other 'necessary' tasks such as ironing, surfing the net, having a cup of tea or a snack, and so on – the recognised skill of creative avoidance, finding things to do to fill the time when we know we should be doing something else. It can result in feelings of lack of fulfilment because you feel you are not achieving as much as you can. This results in stress, unhappiness or even depression.

· Why do we do this? It could be because we are not confident enough to tackle a job on our own and we need to have someone encourage us and give us feedback. Could it be that you have not enough confidence in your own ideas or your ability to make decisions? Or maybe that what you are doing does not appear to help you towards the goals you have in your life – or perhaps it conflicts with the things that you value most. Here are some tips to help you solve this.

- ❖ **Have a structure** to what you do. This will help reduce the number of decisions you need to make. Build into that structure feedback from a trusted friend, colleague or partner if that's important to you.
- ❖ **Find someone to model.** Think of a person who is able to do what it is you find hard to put your mind to. This can be a living person you know personally or it can be a character from fiction or history. Put yourself into their shoes. What would they do? How would they do it? What would they say – how would they say it and to whom? What would they feel about it? This can have an amazing effect on your motivation.
- ❖ **Check out your goals.** Maybe you are not clear about what's important to you, so check these out and be clear about what you want. This will offer you a renewed sense of Purpose and enthusiasm, and therefore add to your happiness.

WORK BOOK

Workbook Step 6 - Purpose

Guide to using the Workbook

When you are going through this Workbook, you will find some of the questions easier than others. Sometimes the answers will spring instantly to mind. Other times you may need to take time out to reflect and consider what this could mean for you.

You may find it useful to go through a checklist of the areas that could affect your answers. When answering these questions, think about what meaning and Purpose the following areas contribute to your life and happiness:

- ❖ your relationships
- ❖ your money
- ❖ your work
- ❖ your health.

This is about being more of who you already are and seeing where happiness lies.

A What are the **three** things that give the greatest Purpose and meaning to your life?

1 ....
   ....
   ....

2 ....
....
....

3 ....
....
....

B Name **three** things that you do for other people, just out of kindness.

1 ....
....
....

2 ....
....
....

3 ....
....
....

C What are **three** things that you could do for others that you don't do now?

1 ....
....
....

2 ....
....
....

3 ....
....
....

Think hard about what you have written above. Decide now what actions you will take that will give your life renewed meaning and, therefore, add to your happiness. Make sure you write them down.

Actions

....

....

....

The Happiness Challenge for Step 6 on the Stairway of Happiness – Purpose

THE HAPPINESS MANTRA

Your happiness state will only change if you do things differently and if you increase the number of Happiness Habits you develop. Remember it takes only 21 days to create permanent change.

In order to increase your happiness, take the Happiness Challenge. Take one of the actions that you have identified in this Workbook. Every day for 21 days, stop just thinking about making this change. Go out and do it!

New habit to be developed

....

....

....

Keep a check on your progress. Put a tick in the box every day for 21 days when you have practised that habit.

Progress Chart						
Day 1	Day 2	Day 3	Day 4	Day 5	Day 6	Day 7
Day 8	Day 9	Day 10	Day 11	Day 12	Day 13	Day 14
Day 15	Day 16	Day 17	Day 18	Day 19	Day 20	Day 21

Start date ....

Appendix 1

Happiness and work

For most of us, the majority of our time is spent at work. A critical ingredient of our happiness therefore is how much we enjoy our working environment, our working relationships and how much the job that we do satisfies our ambition and our skills. The money that we earn will either allow us to live the life that we want to, free from anxieties about debt and bills, or it will fail to give us what we need to do what we truly want.

If you ask people why they are doing the job that they are doing, not many will say that where they are is where they set out to be. Some people have a clear vocation and work with great certainty towards the job that they know they are destined to do. Doctors, teachers, nurses, dentists, clerics of all religious denominations, vets, entrepreneurs are all people who fall into the category of having chosen something specifically that they know they want to do.

However, many of us have just fallen into a role because life's path, coincidence, opportunities just led us to where we are. This

189

could mean that we are now doing something exciting that we love. It could also mean that we really think about our work carefully, we realise that we are not doing what we want to do. We are dissatisfied with the job, the people we are working with, the money that we are being paid and the future career prospects that might await us.

This may mean that you are just jogging along, not consciously unhappy but not loving what you do. When you wake up in the morning, are you looking forward to the day ahead or are you counting the days to your next day off? Think what it could be like if you loved your job and if you were truly realising your potential.

Fill in the Happiness and Work questionnaire to evaluate just how you feel about your job and see whether it is contributing to your overall feeling of happiness. The real challenge will then lie in what you decide to do about it!

Happiness and Work Questionnaire

	Totally agree	Agree	Disagree	Strongly disagree
Culture				
1 My company values me	O	O	O	O
2 My contribution to the business is important	O	O	O	O
3 Where I work is a pleasant place	O	O	O	O
4 I enjoy working in the office	O	O	O	O
Relationships				
1 My boss and I get on well together	O	O	O	O
2 I am part of an excellent team	O	O	O	O
3 I like the people I work with	O	O	O	O
4 The people I work with value me	O	O	O	O

	Totally agree	Agree	Disagree	Strongly disagree

Job content

	Totally agree	Agree	Disagree	Strongly disagree
1 My job is exciting and demanding	○	○	○	○
2 I love what I do	○	○	○	○
3 Every day brings a new challenge	○	○	○	○
4 I know I do a good job	○	○	○	○

Personal growth

	Totally agree	Agree	Disagree	Strongly disagree
1 I am always learning new things	○	○	○	○
2 I will be doing a different job in 5 years' time	○	○	○	○
3 I know more today than I did last year	○	○	○	○
4 I can see 2 career steps with my current company	○	○	○	○

Salary

	Totally agree	Agree	Disagree	Strongly disagree
1 I am happy with what I earn	○	○	○	○
2 I am being paid what I am worth	○	○	○	○
3 I earn enough for my needs	○	○	○	○
4 My salary compares favourably with my peers	○	○	○	○

Satisfaction

	Totally agree	Agree	Disagree	Strongly disagree
1 I look forward to going to work	○	○	○	○
2 I work because I enjoy it	○	○	○	○
3 Work is an important part of my life	○	○	○	○
4 My working day flies by	○	○	○	○

Scoring chart

Now take a pen and count up your scores. Award the points as follows:

Totally agree – 1 point
Agree – 2 points
Disagree – 3 points
Strongly disagree – 4 points

Score	1–24	BAND A
Score	25–48	BAND B
Score	49–72	BAND C
Score	73–96	BAND D

BAND A

You are that fortunate person who is in an exciting job that brings you a lot of personal satisfaction. You like what you are doing and you like who you are doing it with. This rewarding role means that you are enthusiastic about your working life. It is bringing you more than money. You feel you are growing as a person, you are valued and respected, and you can see a future in your company.

BAND B

In general you like your job and the people you are working with. You have a few small distractions with what you are doing, however, so you would benefit from taking the time to decide where you need to bring about change. Does the problem lie with your boss, your colleagues, your salary or are you having doubts about your future with the company? Get to grips with this before it becomes an issue of importance.

BAND C

Life does not seem very happy for you in the world of work. Have you stopped to consider what it is you actually enjoy in your job? Is it something you can deal with or do you need to reconsider who you work for and who you work with? Are they people you could ever get to like and respect? Maybe you are just not getting paid enough? What can you do to increase your earning power? Do you need to retrain and gain extra skills? Take time to reflect on what is important to you in the world of work and what it is you are not getting.

BAND D

You just hate what you do, so what makes you stay there? Have you got the courage and the confidence to find something different? You spend most of your life at work, so why not choose to work in a place where you are with people you like doing something that you enjoy. Happiness will elude you if you don't get to grips with this fundamentally important part of life.

Appendix 2

Find out why older people overall are less happy than younger people.

Lancaster University research findings on the causes of unhappiness

The Participants

18 to 25-year-olds – Younger people
26 to 49-year-olds – Mature people
50+ year-olds – Older people

General

Lack of belonging
Older people are over three times as likely as mature people to experience unhappiness because of feelings of not belonging.

Money
Sixty per cent of people in all age groups felt they were not good with money and that this caused them unhappiness.

Mature people are four times as likely as young people to believe that overspending and debt cause them unhappiness

Surroundings

Weather
Weather is important to people's happiness levels. Bad weather makes people feel unhappy. Good weather also affects people's moods and generally makes them feel happier.

Health
Good health does not give you happiness – you take it for granted. Poor health makes you unhappy whether it's your own ill-health or someone else's.

World problems
Older people are four times as likely to feel unhappy about world problems such as wars and terrorism as young people are.

Lack of control over circumstances
Older people are almost twice as likely as young people to feel unhappy because they are being swept along by events and circumstances.

Behaviour

Emotions
We get more frustrated, anxious and unhappy the older we get. Older people are twice as likely to feel anxiety, frustration and anger as young people.

Eating habits
Older people are twice as likely to be unhappy because of their eating habits than mature people.

Skills and Capabilities

Intelligence levels

Mature people are three times as likely as older people to feel unhappy about their level of intelligence when compared to others.

Opportunities for self-development

Older people are almost half as likely as mature people to believe that their opportunities for self-development are reduced. This can be a source of real unhappiness.

Creativity

Older people are twice as likely to be unhappy about their lack of creativity, musical or artistic ability as mature people.

Missed opportunities

Older people were more than twice as likely to consider missed opportunities as a source of unhappiness than mature people.

Qualifications

Mature people are twice as likely to view lack of qualifications as a source of unhappiness as older people.

Identity

Body image

Older people worry three times as much as mature people about their body image and this adversely affects their happiness levels.

Roots

Mature people are five times as likely as older people to be unhappy about not having any roots.

Purpose

Un-fulfilment

Almost twice as many older people are unhappy because of feelings of un-fulfilment compared to mature people.

Mature people are more than twice as likely as older people to feel that there is no meaning to life. This is a source of unhappiness.

Index